PERSONALITIES AND POLICIES

Essays on English and European History

Presented in Honor
of
Dr. Marguerite Potter

Edited by
E. Deanne Malpass

Introduction by
R. John Rath

TEXAS CHRISTIAN UNIVERSITY PRESS
FORT WORTH, TEXAS

FIRST PRINTING

Library of Congress Catalog Card No. 76-43381
Manufactured in the United States of America

Dr. Marguerite Potter

Preface

This volume is composed of essays by colleagues and former students of Dr. Marguerite Potter. Although scholarly in approach, they are designed to appeal to a wide range of readers. This style seems particularly suitable in a festschrift honoring Dr. Potter since she has strongly supported the American commitment to mass education.

She has taught numerous students that history deepens perception and enlightens the citizenry. Through the interaction of men and their ideas, the personalities and policies of an era, Dr. Potter has convinced many that history is both exciting and challenging. She has communicated year after year her belief that a liberal arts education serves, in Will Durant's words, as "an accumulation, a treasure house of arts and wisdom, manners and morals from which the individual draws nourishment for his mental life."

The people listed on the next pages, as well as others whose names do not appear, made possible the publication of this collection. The editor wishes to express deep thanks to Dr. Marguerite Potter's friends for bringing this project to completion. Particular appreciation is due the Department of History at Texas Christian University.

E. Deanne Malpass
Autumn, 1976

Donors

Myrna Agerton
Dr. Thomas Auffenberg
Dr. Virginia Amos
Nora Anderson
Ruth Van Angell
Lt. Thomas E. Angle
Richard Bailey
Fredona Baker
Mrs. Bruce R. Barrett
Joseph M. Bearden
Alann P. Bedford
Mrs. Joseph D. Biesi
Anna Bines
Mr. and Mrs. M. E. Bobo
Mike Brantley
Jimmie K. Bratton
Barry Broughton
Danny D. Burns
Maxine Burns
Cecilia Burtschi
Eula Lee Carter
Mr. and Mrs. L. Moffitt Cecil
Mrs. Etheridge Holmes Charn
Professor and Mrs. Rawlins Cherryhomes
Dr. and Mrs. Comer Clay
Mary Magee Cobb
Dr. and Mrs. Landon A. Colquitt
Capt. and Mrs. Robert Comolli
Mrs. Ed. W. Compton
David R. Copeland
Virginia Peeler Cothran
Anthony R. Cueto
Jean Ann Daiker
Mr. and Mrs. F. W. Durham Jr.
Dr. Jane E. Dysart
Fran Jurine Edmiston
Mrs. Henry Ellis
Epsilon Eta of Alpha Gamma Delta
Linda J. Ewen
Dr. and Mrs. Macel D. Ezell
Mary Charlotte Faris
Clifford Farmer
First Texas Council of Campfire Girls
Mrs. Beeman Fisher
Oscar and Adele Frazier
Mrs. Bill Forney, Sr.
Mr. and Mrs. Fred H. Fues
Mr. and Mrs. Hal M. Fulfer
John and Darlene Gibbs
Mr. and Mrs. Morris Grimwood
Louise T. Grisham
David R. Hall
James A. Hall
Mr. and Mrs. M. G. Hamilton
Dr. Nancy Ailene Harder
Dena M. Hardwick
Patricia Ann Hardy
Mr. and Mrs. A. J. Harlan
Elvira H. Harris
Julia Magee Hartley
Thomas E. Hicks
Dr. Lawrence W. Hill
Foye Hodnett
Mr. and Mrs. Robert Holt
Jeff and Martha Horn
Mr. and Mrs. Russell Howland
William A. Hudson
Mr. and Mrs. R. W. Hughes
Ruth Huston
Mr. and Mrs. James H. W. Jacks

Dr. and Mrs. Jere Jackson
Mr. and Mrs. Ted R. Jamison, Sr.
Dr. and Mrs. Ted R. Jamison, Jr.
Lorene Jay
Margrit Jay
Thurman and Claudia Jay
T. L. Jay
Burna Jolley
Mary C. Jones
Alla Roy E. Kergthentall
James W. Kerr, Jr.
Mr. and Mrs. Joe Kilchenstein
Mr. & Mrs. Walter W. Killough
Dr. and Mrs. Roy U. T. Kim
Dr. and Mrs. Gene Kirkpatrick
Margaret Kitts
Frankie Mae Krog
Mr. and Mrs. Joseph Lake
Mrs. Baxter Lee
Frien D. Lee
Sherri Parker Lee
Dr. Edwin E. Lehr
Mr. and Mrs. J. B. Lovejoy
Julie Macune
Mrs. S. A. Mahaffey
Mr. and Mrs. Alton Tate Malpass
E. Deanne Malpass
Rosemari Martin
Ruth E. Martin
Mr. and Mrs. Bob Massie
Dr. Ralph F. Massie, M.D.
Pauline K. Mathis
Dr. Linda Lee Maxwell
Fay Maberry
Dr. and Mrs. C. K. McFarland
Dr. Thomas N. McGaffey
Beth Ann McGaffey
Dr. and Mrs. Malcolm D. McLean
Paula McPheeters
Margaret McWhorter
Mary J. Mendon
Leon Mitchell, Jr.
Alla Ray Morris
Chancellor and Mrs. James M. Moudy
Mrs. Karl Mueller
Mrs. A. F. Murph
Dr. Lawrence Murphy
Dr. and Mrs. Nevin E. Neal
Dr. and Mrs. James Newcomer
Miss L. A. Norr
Mr. and Mrs. Fred B. Norris
Dr. and Mrs. W. C. Nunn
Mr. and Mrs. Frank D. Olin
Edward J. Owen
Richard D. Owen
The Reverend William Parkey
Frances G. Peadon
Charles L. Peveler
Mary Lee Poindexter
Mr. and Mrs. Carl K. Potter
David and Linda Potter
Jewel Carr Potter
Frances Powell
Lillian Preston
Mrs. R. L. Proffer
A. S. Puddles
Mrs. Frank (Pat) Quattrochi
Mrs. Karl Ratliff
Hilton T. Ray
Dr. and Mrs. H. S. Renshaw
Mr. and Mrs. J. S. Renshaw
Dr. and Mrs. Olin C. Robison
Dr. and Mrs. E. Leigh Secrest
Dr. and Mrs. Wendell G. Schaffer
Ira J. Schantz
Patricia Penrose Schieffer
Janet L. Schmelzer
Mr. and Mrs. Steve Schuster
Mrs. Evelyn Schwier
Hallye E. Schwier
Daniel G. Shackelford
Dr. Lorraine Sherley
Milton and Elsie Skeen
Mrs. Dott Edward Smith
Mrs. Mary Grace Smith
Mr. and Mrs. Robert P. Smith
Dr. and Mrs. Karl E. Snyder
Arlene L. Sollenberger
Gail M. Sones
Mr. and Mrs. Everett V. Staudt
Barbara Evans Stewart
Stevi Anne Stites
Charles Edward Stuart
Dr. and Mrs. Jaime Suchlicki
Carrie L. Tate
Dr. and Mrs. Robert M. Taylor

TCU Travel Board
Annie Jo Thaxton
Mr. and Mrs. C. A. Thompson
Maybelle Tinkle
Mr. and Mrs. J. M. Tippett
James and Susan Tippett
Grace Van Tine
Maurice Van Tine
Paul Van Tine
Ruth Potter Van Tine
Dr. and Mrs. Herndon Wagers
Anne Walker
Mrs. Bert Walker
Dr. and Mrs. Granville Walker
Mr. and Mrs. Harry Wandry
P. Warbeck
Dr. and Mrs. James R. Ward
Dr. and Mrs. Paul Wassenich
Mrs. C. R. F. Wickenden
Mr. and Mrs. W. Erskine Williams
Dr. and Mrs. Maurice Williams
J. Don Williamson
Jack and Robbie A. Wilson
John F. Wilson
Dr. and Mrs. C. Carr Winn
Dr. and Mrs. Donald E. Worcester
Mr. and Mrs. James H. Wood
Mrs. Carla Wright
Sadie Wright
Mr. and Mrs. R. B. Yanaway
Carol and John Yocom
Mrs. C. D. Yost

Table of Contents

Illustrations

(All plates immediately follow page 12.)

Introduction[1]

This volume is a tribute by colleagues and former students to a modest, although not meek, scholar, lecturer, teacher, gourmet cook, world traveler, embroiderer, and friend, whose exemplary virtues as a great teacher have deeply affected the personal, academic, and professional lives of many people.

Marguerite Potter, member of the Department of History at Texas Christian University since 1944, can be counted among the handful of truly great teachers. Even though her courses in British history for years have had the reputation of being among the toughest in the whole university, her lectures are so colorful, lively, witty, intelligent, and provocative that her classes are always packed to capacity. Her standards are exacting, and she expects every student to read and master every page of assigned material, but her requirements are always clear. At the beginning of the term some students have found her austere, even terrifying, but they have always found her interesting. Beginning her lectures exactly on time, she organizes her material so carefully that she never uses a note and finishes the topic under discussion precisely at the end of the period. Dr. Potter throws so many facts at her students during the intervening minutes that, in the words of one of them, "If you drop your pencil in class, before you can pick it up and start writing again you're behind fifty years."

It is obvious that part of Professor Potter's success as a teacher can be attributed to her impressive knowledge of the literature in a wide variety of fields. She did not attain this proficiency, as did Ananias Twist's typical Texans, by reading books because their "television sets are broken" or by dropping "into a well heated library on a cold day or an air-conditioned reading room on a hot one, while [waiting] for their husband or wife to get out of the barber shop or the beauty parlor."[2] Dr. Potter, a Missourian by birth, fell in love with books in her grandfather's big library on a farm not far from Sedalia, Missouri. It was here and in grade school and high school that she memorized much of the poetry and mastered some of the genealogical facts that she intersperses in her lectures and seminar discussions. Her skills in other endeavors such as book reviewing, writing poetry, directing tours, coaching the nationally televised College Bowl team, cooking, crewel embroidery, and distributing hand mirrors during a self-study program at her university were learned at a less tender age.

Somehow I suspect that indefatigable energy and much hard work lie behind many of the attainments of the faculty member in whose honor this festschrift is written. At least she labored energetically enough when writing her doctoral thesis at the University of Texas and she managed to "hold the good thought" long enough to convince her supervising professor that he personally should pick up the chapters at her apartment as they were completed and return them to her with his comments and suggestions on how the manuscript could possibly be improved. Her supervisor will always remember her during her Austin, Texas, days as a well organized, efficient, energetic young lady surrounded by books and research notes methodically piled on stacks all over her desk and the floor adjacent to it. She was too much of a perfectionist to follow the advice which she reputedly gives some of her own graduate students:"Good Gussie! Get on with it! You ain't writing no masterpiece." (She turned out a real masterpiece!)

Although Professor Potter has literally terrorized graduate students unacquainted with her basically kind nature into believing that she expects them to work as hard as she does, she always wins them over through her impressive mastery of her field, her fairness, thoughtfulness, kindness, sense of humor, and legendary culinary feats. When graduate students go to her home, they repeatedly demonstrate their devotion to their hostess by playing with Bonnie Prince Charles, in spite of the fact that they may be allergic to dogs. After she once suggested that her lawn needed landscaping they all showed up, in part because they knew that later on they would have another one of Potter's renowned gourmet dinners.

The influence of the person to whom this volume has been

dedicated extends much further than the Texas Christian University community. One of the most popular lecturers in Fort Worth, she has emphasized the necessity of giving students a liberal education and has expressed her fear that although we are training a generation of experts, we are not providing our youth with any basis for moral judgments, thereby making them ready victims of extremists on both the left and the right. If Copernicus, Galileo, or Newton walked into the science laboratories of a modern university, she has ventured to say, they would be lost because our scientific knowledge has advanced so far during the past two centuries. "But if Socrates or Jesus came to talk about moral values, too many students would not understand them."

Professor Potter has published numerous book reviews and scholarly papers as well as two books: *Grass-Roots Diplomat: Neville G. Penrose, Buen Amigo y Vecino* (1961); and *Snide Lights on Texas History* (1959), which was written in collaboration with Dr. William C. Nunn under the pseudonym of Ananias Twist. She is now working on a volume dealing with British foreign policy during the Italo-Ethiopian crisis. Her colleagues have accorded her long-deserved recognition for outstanding leadership in the fields of British and European history by electing her chairman of the history section of the Southwestern Social Science Association, a member of the executive board of the National Conference on British Studies, and president of the Southern Conference on British Studies.

The planning of the present volume as a tribute to her by countless former and present students and other friends and the thoughtful and well researched essays in it bear ample testimony to the fact that Marguerite Potter has earned the admiration and devotion of many people.

R. John Rath*

*Dr. Rath is Mary Gibbs Jones Professor of History at Rice University.

Notes

[1]The author wishes to thank numerous students, colleagues, and friends of Professor Potter for providing him with the information on which many of the facts in this introduction are based.

[2]As quoted from Robert Stephenson Lewis' *Pieces of Mind* by Ananias Twist in his *Snide Lights on Texas History* (San Antonio, Texas: The Naylor Company, 1959), p. 71.

1

Sir Thomas More and the Defense of the Royal Navy

by
R. Morris Day
East Tennessee State University

The summer's day broke fair over the great harbor and naval base of Brest on August 10, 1512. Off Pointe de St. Mathieu, two leagues from the entrance to the harbor, the main French fleet of some thirty warships under the command of René de Clermont, Vice-Admiral of France, rode at anchor. It was St. Lawrence's Day, the feastday of one of the seven deacons of Rome, who was martyred in 258, legend has it, by being roasted alive over a grid. On board the warships the celebration was beginning, and many gentlemen had their wives and ladies with them for the festivities.

Across the Channel, however, the English naval base of Portsmouth lay in silence. Only days before, the port had hummed with the excitement of fitting out the fleet. Boats plied back and forth, carrying their loads of victuals (beer, biscuit, beef, and fish), powder and shot, and other armaments to the warships riding in the Solent. Coming down to Portsmouth in early August, the king himself inspected the fleet and, finding everything in order, gave a banquet for his admiral and captains. As the courses followed one another and the wine goblets were refilled, each captain rose to swear before God and king that he would come to the aid of his brother captains and then, "with great noyse of minstrelsie,"[1] took boat for his ship. Henry VIII rode back north satisfied that his navy would acquit itself well while masters kept a wary eye aloft, waiting for the green and white pennants to stream out in the direction of France.

With the first wind the fleet sailed, and at the moment the French were preparing for their celebration the great ships and their lighter escorts lumbered through the seas toward Brest. Under the command of Sir Edward Howard, the victor over the

Barton brothers in the famous action of 1511, the fleet sailed as armies marched — in three divisions: the van, the battle or the center, and the rear.

It was the first year of the War of the Holy League, one of the first wars of the Renaissance, which pitted Pope Julius II, Ferdinand of Spain, and Henry VIII against the Valois king of France, Louis XII. Some would call it an unholy alliance, and indeed the motives of the allies were as mixed as they were selfish. Having all but accomplished his objective of reducing Venice "to its original condition of a fishing village,"[2] the pope now looked on with apprehension as Castile, his former ally in the war against the maritime republic, Venice, threatened papal territories. Ferdinand the Fox cast covetous eyes on Navarre, and needing a diversion in the north to keep the French occupied, brought in his son-in-law as an ally. For his part, Henry VIII was only too happy to oblige. Young and arrogant, steeped in the stories of Henry V, victor of Agincourt, and burning with the desire to emulate him, Henry VIII had scarcely adjusted the crown to his head when he was threatening war with France. Indeed he was boasting of war before the crown touched his head. In May, 1509, one month before the coronation, William Blount, Lord Mountjoy, wrote Erasmus that with the coming of the new king liberal patronage of scholars would be the order of the day, for as Henry had declared, England "could hardly live without them." But in the same month Marino Sanuto the Younger, Secretary to the Venetian Senate, noted a routine diplomatic dispatch from London and wrote in his diary that Henry VII was dead and Henry VIII had sworn to make war on France immediately. Sanuto the Venetian fathomed Henry's intentions much more clearly than did Mountjoy the Englishman. A few months after his coronation Henry so openly insulted the French ambassador that the latter left the court, and a few days after this incident the king wrote Ferdinand, inquiring as to how long peace would have to be maintained with France.[3]

To start a war required patience and planning, replied Ferdinand. So chafing at the bit, Henry used the few years of peace to strengthen the Royal Navy, until in 1512 Ferdinand decided that the time was ripe for Henry to keep the French engaged while he conquered Navarre. Unaware of Ferdinand's treacherous designs, perhaps not caring, Henry prepared enthusiastically for the renewal of the Hundred Years War. During the spring of 1512, while the English army was being mobilized, Henry unleashed the fleet against the French. With seventeen warships under his command Howard swept the Channel in April — "skowered the sea," Hall put it[4] — taking some twelve to fourteen prizes and meeting with no opposition. In May the army under Thomas Grey, Marquis of Dorset, converged on Southampton, where the transports waited. In early June the heavy warship *Regent*, having completed her victualling, took her place in the fleet, bringing its strength to eighteen warships. Shortly thereafter Howard put to sea once again, escorting the troop-laden transports down the Channel. After clearing the Breton peninsula he broke off the escort and took up a cruising station that placed him between the convoy making its way into the Bay of Biscay and the French naval base. Satisfied after three days that the transports were free from any danger, he bearded the lion in its den, taking the fleet into Brest, where English landing parties put the torch to the scattered villages. As smoke darkened the countryside and no evidence of opposition of any sort could be seen, influential citizens of the area, despairing of any support from Louis XII, came on board the English flagship to ask for a truce. He was sent "hither to make warre and not peace,"[5] Howard replied, but nevertheless left the coast a few days thereafter to search for a French fleet reported to be at sea. The report was in error, but while no French warships were sighted, Howard managed to intercept two merchant fleets, capturing some forty prizes before returning to port with the fleet.

Thus far the English fleet had encountered no opposition. But the war was only beginning, and already ominous signs indicated that it was not to be a summertime lark in France. From the north came intelligence that the Scots, remaining true to tradition, would soon enter the war as an ally of France. From the south came nothing but Ferdinand's empty promises that the aid specified by treaty would soon arrive. From Fontarabia news arrived that the idle English army, unsupported by the Spanish, was nearing a state of mutiny. And last, from all sides came reports that the French fleet was being fitted out, as was that of the Scots, and that the English would soon face a combined fleet.

Undaunted by the sobering news, Henry resolved to strike

first. The navy would attack the French in their home base in preparation for the crossing of an even greater English army under the dreaded "el Thalabot," George Talbot, Earl of Shrewsbury, and in July the fleet was revictualled for the coming campaign.

Thus it was that when the English fleet loomed into sight an hour before noon on St. Lawrence's Day, the French were caught by surprise. On paper the two fleets were about equal. The French fleet numbered about thirty ships; the English, which had been increased in strength during the summer, between twenty-five and thirty. Individual ship strength was also about equal. *Regent*, rated at 1,000 tons, was the Goliath of both fleets, but the French *Grande Louise* and *Cordelière* were rated at 790 and 700 tons respectively. Captains with experience commanded on both sides, and indeed, Hervé de Porzmoguer, captain of *Cordelière*, had already gained such a reputation for plundering, that on the June raid, around Berthram Bay, Howard had specifically ordered Porzmoguer's house burned.[6]

Despite the matched odds, however, the French hurriedly made sail in an attempt to regain the protection of the fortifications at Brest. But the heavier French warships could not get underway quickly enough, and like a hawk diving into a flock of chickens the English were upon them, opening fire together so that the cannonade was so fierce "all the sea coast sounded of it."[7] A general melée ensued. Howard, flying his flag in the new ship, *Mary Rose*, singled out his opposite number, Clermont's *Grande Louise*, and the heavy guns of the Henrican ship did their job so well and so quickly that Clermont broke off the engagement and fled toward the sanctuary of the harbor, claiming later that his mainmast had been shot away. At the same time, *Sovereign* engaged *Cordelière*, inflicting considerable damage, but either as a result of the smoke, which obscured vision, or because of miscalculation on the part of her master, the English ship sheered off to the stern, carrying her out of the action. *Mary James*, under the command of Anthony Ughtred, was already coming up, however, pouring a devastating fire into *Cordelière* from her six heavy curtals, when Sir Anthony Knynet's *Regent*, which had been closely engaged with *Dieppe* commanded by Rigault de Berquetot, came to the aid of *Sovereign* and *Mary James* and succeeded in grappling *Cordelière*. The fighting was savage. Almost immediately Knynet was killed in the heavy exchange between guns and crossbows. The English nevertheless finally succeeded in boarding *Cordelière*, fighting their way over the decks of the ships, driving the French, encumbered as they were by the presence of wives and ladies, before them.

What happened next is debated. Seeing the English so close to victory, the chronicler Hall declared, a French gunner, preferring "to die a heretic," fired the magazine. Other reports had it that a shot from *Mary James* reached the powder casks. Whatever the cause, flames quickly swept the French ship, but *Regent* could not disengage. Soon she was afire also, and the two great ships, locked in a death embrace by the grappling irons like two great stags with antlers entwined, turned slowly around stern to stern, as the flames fed on wood and canvas, turning them into a floating furnace. So intense was the heat that English rescue boats could not come close to the two ships and, as a result, less than two hundred men were saved — 180 from *Regent*, only six from *Cordelière*. Porzmoguer was not among the survivors, a witness reporting that he had jumped overboard in full armor and was drowned. As the smoke billowed up to hang over the anchorage like palls from a funeral pyre—an ironic end to the celebration of St. Lawrence's Day—Berquetot made good his escape in *Dieppe* after fighting a furious action against several English warships. The first battle of Brest was over.[8]

Both admirals claimed victory. Calling a council of his captains, Howard boosted their sagging morale and then for several days raided along the Breton coast, burning everything in sight — in effect, daring the French to come out and fight. When it was obvious that the French were content to remain penned up in Brest, Howard sailed for home. Even before his arrival Henry VIII had appointed Howard Lord Admiral of England to replace the deceased Earl of Oxford. Now the king rewarded his new admiral with a reward of £66 for good service. Both swore vengeance for *Regent*. Henry VIII would build a new ship bigger than any ever before seen; Howard would, he vowed before God, "nevyr se the Kyng in the face tyl he hath revengyd the deth of the Nobyll and valyant sir Thomas Knynet."[9]

On the French side Clermont reported to Louis XII that he had won a great victory and, as a result of the good news received a reward of 100 francs. But Clermont's victory—if such it could be called — soon turned sour. Berquetot, supported by all of his brother captains, accused Clermont of cowardice, challenging his admiral to a judicial combat. The duel was never fought. Instead, Louis XII held an official inquiry, the controversy was glossed over, and, although Clermont was temporarily disgraced, he nevertheless retained his command.

Filed away to molder, perhaps lost, Clermont's reports, which led Louis XII to boast that one French ship could confound the entire British fleet, have never been unearthed. Probably, however—and *probably* must be emphasized—Clermont's falsehoods lived on, undeservedly, in Renaissance epic poetry. Following the battle, with the intention of commemorating the supposed French victory, Germanus Brixius (Germain de Brie), humanist, friend of Erasmus and confessor to Queen Anne of Brittany, wife of Louis XII and his patron, wrote a short neo-Vergilian epic poem of 344 lines describing the heroic struggle of a brave captain and his ship as well as their tragic destruction (*Cordelière* had been owned by Queen Anne). *Chordigerae Navis Conflagratio* was a fluent Latin poem, anticipating the elegance of neoclassism. Unfortunately, the facts were patently in error, raising "the classic Renaissance question of poetic license versus poetic liars."[10]

In building Hervé into an epic hero and reversing the roles of pursuer and pursued, Brixius distorted the real outlines of the battle.

> Nor did the numberous crowd of English sail
> Covering all the sea, make Hervé's courage fail —
> At once prepared upon the foe to dash,
> To move in broadside, ready for a clash,
> Forward he steers amidst the waves, and takes
> *Cordelière* where th' open ocean breaks;
> She flies, and (as they come) each shattered ship
> She sends down deep beneath the waves to dip.
> The *Regent*, England's chief ship, next in sight
> With its tail turned, she follows, puts to flight.
> The *Regent* flees on course, outstrips the gale.
> But ours gives chase; impelled by seamen hale

And hearty, helped by Captain Hervé's cheer,
She's swifter, and relentlessly must steer
Hard on the *Regent's* side, and grapple her near.

If this were not enough to offend English honor, Brixius went right on to introduce a simile that was even more distasteful, comically comparing *Regent* to a rabbit fleeing for its life:

Thus when a hound pursues a hare in flight,
Which flees from rage, escapes the empty bite,
Pell-mell flies on through open field;
The dog its destin'd prey will never yield,
Clings to the rabbit's neck with each fang bare —
In greedy bite, it takes the hasting hare.

With victory snatched from the jaws of the hound by the terrible fire, again a reversal of fact, only the gods can end the battle. Rather than Howard's penning the French in Brest Harbor, Zeus must send a storm:

The driving rains sweep on, the thunder raves,
The bounding waters pound, with crashing waves
The broad seas roar, in downpours from on high
The sea invades the dense, cloud-hidden sky.
You'd think all Heav'n descending in the deep,
You'd think th' ascending sea Heav'n's height did steep.[11]

In the heat of the war, and it grew even hotter in 1513, Thomas More, then undersheriff of London, his ability as a lawyer already established and his literary and political stars on the rise, replied to the poem in a series of Latin epigrams. More wrote that the lack of reality in Brixius' painting of a dog and a rabbit was so astonishing that the painter had to resort to the label, "this is the dog; this is the rabbit." In another epigram he portrayed the poet as a liar, celebrating "on the subject of the ship *Cordelière*, a thousand lies which are the very opposite of the facts." Nor, continued More, was he surprised that in his [Brixius'] "vicious prejudice he deliberately determined to record lies." Consequently, the poet "deserved to be aboard — amidships — so that he might know the whole story more accurately."

With that, More had fired his starboard broadside and, without hesitation, he came about to bring his port guns to bear. He ridiculed the hero, Hervé, as well as the poet. As the fighting began, Brixius had Hervé deliver a thirty-line oration in behalf of queen and country, buttressed with references to the patriots of republican Rome—the Fabii, Decii, and Curtii. Then as the battle was joined, Hervé fought with almost superhuman powers, wielding a formidable array of weapons against the English. But in vain, for as the ships caught fire, rendering victory impossible, he accepted the inevitable. In a twenty-three line epic speech, Hervé urged his men to die bravely, telling them that the flames will purge them as St. Lawrence was purged, and thus secure in heaven they will endure on earth, for a poet of ability [Brixius] will record their deeds in song. Only a man with five hands, More wrote, could fight as Hervé had done; therefore, "he was a strange monster, frightful for both his grimace and his strength." If, furthermore, he continued, "our age has only Hervé to compare to the two Decii, then remember this difference: the Decii died willingly; Hervé, because he could not avoid it." With the hero considerably reduced in stature, More aimed the final gun at the author "of that overgrown little poem which recounts the feats and death of the warrior Hervé," accusing Brixius of plagiarism. "O blessed poetical skill—and yet whoever, by the kind of skill you have, lends freshness to what is old, at the same time, where he has no skill (sweat though he may), imposes senescence on what is new."[13]

More's attack was no more just than Brixius' rendering of history. Recognizing this unfairness, perhaps, or allowing the humanist to reassert himself over the nationalist — though humanism and nationalism were not all incompatible in the Renaissance — he put Brixius and the poem from his mind. The epigrams were not published. The quarrel remained a private matter between More and his pen, forgotten as the war continued. True to his promise after the *Regent-Cordelière* fight, Henry VIII built an even greater warship, *Henry Grace à Dieu*, and with the English armies faring badly, himself led the army to France in 1513, winning a battle of sorts and capturing Tournai, while his queen Catherine destroyed the Scottish army. True to his promise also, Howard sought his revenge for the death of

Regent's captain and died in a desperate fight aboard one of Prégent de Bidoux's galleys in the second battle of Brest, 25 April, 1513. The next year the war ground to a halt. Having conquered Navarre, Ferdinand had long since deserted Henry, making a separate truce with France. The same year in Rome the warlike Julius II had gone to his reward—excluded from heaven, Erasmus wrote in *Julius Exclusus*—and the new pope, Leo X, sought peace. In 1514 the treaty was signed, sealed by the marriage of Henry's sister, Mary, to Louis XII. If Henry VIII had won no Agincourts, at least he had suffered no Bouvines.

But the edifice of English victory quickly crumbled, despite Wolsey's efforts to keep the peace. Events of great magnitude followed one another too rapidly. In January, 1515, Louis XII died. The Tudor-Valois alliance was thus dissolved, and even more important, the new king, Francis I, was a French version of Henry VIII. Before the end of his first regnal year he had invaded Italy and actively stirred up the Scots against England. In January, 1516, Ferdinand died, and when his grandson, Charles of Burgundy, succeeded him, two hereditary enemies of the French were forged into one. Still, it seemed that diplomacy might maintain the peace, which, if shaky, nonetheless was peace. Wolsey renewed his efforts and succeeeded in negotiating the Treaty of London, which guaranteed the status quo and was signed by all the major powers. In 1518, however, Maximilian died, and in the bitter contest to succeed him Charles won, thereby placing Spain, Burgundy and the Holy Roman Empire—all enemies of France—under one crown. For France, the situation was intolerable. General war was inevitable. That England could remain neutral was unlikely. The old order, Wolsey's world, had been upended as easily as a chess board kicked over by a drunken man, and in the new order, which was fast unfolding, he had the impossible task of restraining a king who aspired to be a sixteenth century Henry V.[14]

Indeed, despite the wooing of both Francis and Charles, it seems that Henry had long since decided to continue his crusade against France. As early as 1520 Henry and Charles began planning for joint naval operations in case war broke out with France. Later the same year Henry's conference with Francis, amid the splendor of the Field of Cloth of Gold served less to decrease rivalry than to exacerbate jealousy and distrust.

In this tense situation late in 1520 the question of who had told the truth about the *Regent-Cordelière* fight burst out anew — this time in public. The quarrel had surfaced in 1518, when Erasmus published an edition of More's epigrams, including those written against Brixius. Singularly, the anti-Brixius epigrams were witty and devastatingly critical; together in one volume they hit the French humanist like a burst of machine gun fire. Brixius found himself described as a deliberate liar, falsifier of history, plagiarist, and, worst of all, a bad grammarian, as More wished him to have been amidships of *Cordelière*, the implication being to prevent bad poetry from being conceived.

An infuriated Brixius replied with a broadside of his own in *The Antimorus* of 1519. Defending his version of the naval action of 1512, he hung the liar's wreath around More's neck, charged that it was More who was the bad grammarian, citing specific errors (More acknowledged these by correcting most of them in subsequent editions), and then made an accusation that touched a dangerous nerve. Referring to More's laudatory lines on the occasion of Henry VIII's coronation in which criticism was made of the previous reign of Henry VII, Brixius charged More with disloyalty to the Tudors. For More the issue of loyalty was both dangerous and embarrassing — dangerous, because a suspected enemy of the Tudors had slight chance of survival; embarassing, because More was now a servant of the king and a member of the council. The next year, therefore, he replied to the attack in his *Epistola ad Germanus Brixius*. Restating his version of the *Regent-Cordelière* battle, he strongly defended Henry VIII's policies and just as strongly affirmed his loyalty to the dynasty.

With the *Epistola* the war of words ended, drowned out by Henry's preparations for his second French war in which England won little glory and incurred great expense. The revolt against Rome followed and, hard on its heels, a third war with France. By that time More was dead, executed for disloyalty to Henry VIII. In the swirl of events shaking Europe the *Regent-Cordelière* fight was forgotten, as was Brixius and his poem. Sir Thomas More, because he lived on, either as saint to the devout or as a Socratic figure to the more secular-minded, had the last word in defense of one of the first major actions ever fought by the Royal Navy. It is found in his epigram on Brixius, the *Cordelière*, and the *Antimorus*: "Behold, Germanus Brixius, rich in resources on both land and sea, has a forest (*syluam*) and a raft. Do you want to know what advantage each affords him? His stupidities ride the raft, his madness inhabits the forest." The forest (*syluam*) is *Antimorus*, *syluam* being commonly used in Renaissance Latin to indicate a collection of verse. Raft, *ratem*, was the *Cordelière*.[15]

Notes

1. Edward Hall, *Hall's Chronicle; Containing the History of England During the Reign of Henry IV and the Succeeding Monarchs, to the End of the Reign of Henry the Eighth* (London: 1809 ed.), p. 534.
2. Francesco Guicciardini, *The History of Italy*, trans. and ed. by Sidney Alexander (New York: Macmillan Co., 1969), p. 201.
3. *Letters and Papers, Foreign and Domestic, of the Reign of Henry VIII, and Addenda*, ed. by J. S. Brewer, et al. (23 vols.; London: Longmans, 1862-1920), I, 51, 162. Citation by document number, and citations to volume 1 are to the second edition; *Calendar of State Papers Relating to English Affairs, Existing in the Archives and Collections of Venice, and in Other Libraries of Northern Italy*, ed. by Rawdon Brown, et al. (9 vols.; London: Longman and Green, 1864-98), II, 11. Citation by document number.
4. Hall, *Chronicle*, p. 527.
5. Ibid. p. 533.

6. For Henrican warships, see E.H.H. Archibald, *The Wooden Fighting Ship in the Royal Navy, A.D. 897-1860* (New York: Arco Publishing Co., Inc., 1968); P.R.O. SPI/230/201-203-205; and the model of *Great Michael* (126.20), Department of Technology, Royal Scottish Museum, Edinburgh. For the ship list, see R. C. Anderson, *List of English Men-of-War, 1509-1649, The Society of Nautical Research Occasional Publications No. 7* (London: Society for Nautical Research, 1959.) Revisions of this list by Tom Glasgow Jr., R. Morris Day and others, can be found in the *Mariner's Mirror.*
7. Hall, *Chronicle*, p. 534.
8. Alfred A. Spont (ed.), *Letters and Papers Relating to the War with France, 1512-1513* (London: Navy Records Society, 1897), 39. Citation by number; *L. & P., Hen. VIII*, I, 1043.
9. Hall, *Chronicle*, 535; Spont, *Letters & Papers*, 30.
10. For the literary aspects of the poem, I have depended entirely on Harry G. Merrill, "Sea-dogs or Humanists?: The Renaissance Epic and Sir Thomas More." Unpublished paper delivered before the Tennessee Philological Society, 1975. The older work on the subject is H. H. Hudson, *The Epigram in the English Renaissance* (Princeton, N.J.: Princeton University Press, 1949).
11. Germanus Brixius, *Chordigerae Navis Conflagratio* (1514 ed., copy in British Museum), Latin, 11., 29-42, 43-48, 317-322. Translated by Harry G. Merrill.
12. For More, the standard biography is, R. W. Chambers, *Thomas More* (London: Jonathan Cape, 1935).
13. Leicester Bradner and Charles Arthur Lynch (eds. & trs.), *The Latin Epigrams of Thomas More* (Chicago: University of Chicago Press, 1953), nos. 168, 170, 171, 174, 175, 177, 178.
14. See, Garrett Mattingly, "An Early Non-aggression Pact," *The Journal of Modern History*, X (March, 1938), pp. 1-30.
15. Bradner & Lynch, *Epigrams*, no. 251. See also, Brixius, *Anti-Morus* (1519 ed., copy in British Museum) and More, *Epistola ad Germanũ Brixiũ* (1520 ed., copy in the Folger Shakespeare Library).

Plate one

MARY TUDOR, QUEEN OF ENGLAND

by Antonio Moro

Museo del Prado, Madrid

Plate two

THE DWARF OF CHARLES V

by Antonio Moro

Louvre, Paris

Plate three

ANTONIO MORO: SELF PORTRAIT

National Gallery of Art, Washington, D.C.

Plate four

SIR HENRY LEE

by Antonio Moro

National Portrait Gallery, London

2

Mary Tudor's Portrait Painter — Antonio Moro

by
Maurice Boyd
Texas Christian University

Thanks to the marriage of Mary Tudor to Prince Philip of Spain in 1554, the English-speaking world discovered a master court painter. He called himself Antonio Moro, but the Hapsburgs knew him as Antonio Moro van Dashorst. The people of England called him Sir Anthony More, for in 1554 Queen Mary Tudor knighted him.[1]

Among those witnessing the ceremony of knighthood were Prince Philip of Spain, Mary's husband by their recent marriage, and members of his cortege: Bartolomé de Carranza, Spain's representative at the Council of Trent and the Queen's confessor; Alfonso y Castro, Philip's Franciscan chaplain; Juan de Villagarcıa, a noted Spanish Dominican; Simon Renard; the Spanish diplomat known as the Duke of Feria; Ruy Gómez de Silva, Philip's secretary who was later known as the Prince of Eboli, together with his petite one-eyed wife Ana de Mendoza; the powerful Duke of Alba; and the Marquis of Cortez. English representatives included Sir Thomas Gresham; Sir Henry Lee Sydney and wife; Jane Dormer, the Queen's vivacious lady-in-waiting who later became the Duchess of Feria; and many others. The mere whisper of Moro's name produced eulogies concerning his paintings of all these dignitaries, English as well as Spanish, queen as well as king.

Who was this mysterious man bursting suddenly from obscurity amidst the fanfare of trumpets surrounding the royal wedding? From whence came this stranger with the Islamic name?

Antonio Moro was born in Utrecht. Where his parents originated is not known, but in 1517 a Philip Mor received power of attorney from a Dirk Mor, apparently his brother. This same Dirk Mor is mentioned in a sheriff's brief dated 1555 as Dirk Mor van Dashorst. Philip Mor was Antonio Moro's father. Dashorst was a small Burgundian landed estate, and the name was used to distinguish members of this branch of the Mor family from another branch, which called itself van Amersfort. Dirk apparently died without issue, and his estate passed to his nephew Anthonis Mor van Dashorst or Antonio Moro.[2]

Metgen, Antonio Moro's wife, was a widow when he married her in 1542. Their children were a son, Philip, and two daughters: Catherine, who married Jan Casetta, one of the Duke of Alba's most prominent tax collectors in East Flanders; and Elizabeth, who married an attorney named Henri van der Horst.[3]

Antonio Moro studied his craft under Jan Scorel, who had enjoyed the patronage of Pope Adrian VI, a fellow Fleming also from Utrecht.[4] When Scorel returned to Utrecht from Rome after the pope's death in 1524, he distinguished himself through a series of group portraits of Jerusalem pilgrims. By the late 1530's Antonio Moro was already working in Scorel's studio. The 1541 group portrait of the "Five Jerusalem Pilgrims" depicting the canons of Utrecht is at least partly the work of Moro. Because of the pope's interest in his work and the fact that he was a canon of Utrecht, Scorel was able to maintain close relationships with the nobility and upper clergy of the Netherlands. Through Scorel, therefore, Antonio Moro early became acquainted with both the Bishop of Arras — later Cardinal Granvelle — and the regent of the Netherlands, Queen Maria of Hungary, who in turn recommended him to the Emperor Charles V.[5]

Antonio's years of closely supervised apprenticeship and study under Jan Scorel ended in 1542. He had greatly benefitted not only from Scorel's artistic competence, but from his friendships with members of the royalty and high clergy.[6] Scorel's creative genius, evident in his group portraits painted between 1525 and 1535, made him the progenitor of the bourgeois group portrait. Scorel had, nevertheless, pointed Moro toward the "new and superior status unique at a time when artists began to choose between their duties as guildsmen and their obligations to the court."[7] To his master Moro owed many things, but above all the "immaculate perfection to which Moro's portrait painting aspired."[8]

Scorel impressed upon Moro the fact that in portraiture creating an excellent likeness depended upon the careful placing and relative spacing of facial features such as eyes, nose, and mouth. A remarkable and ever-present characteristic of Moro's portraits is that the eyes of the subject contemplate the viewer, and that *without exception* one eye occupies the exact center of the space assigned to the face as a whole.[9] Characteristic features such as these confirm that Moro had found a formula of both artistry and productivity early in his studies under the great Scorel.

Antonio Moro first visited England in 1553 in the entourage of Flemish envoys sent by Emperor Charles V to protect Mary Tudor's claim to the English throne when young King Edward lay dying. Anticipating Philip's journey to the Netherlands on the request of his father, Moro had preceded him there in time to join the Flemish courtiers embarking for England. The opportunity arose for Moro to paint young Edward VI before his death and to present the portrait to Mary Tudor, whom Edward had admired.[10]

One of Charles' Flemish servants, skilled diplomat Simon Renard, was entrusted with the negotiations for Prince Philip's marriage to Mary Tudor. Since Mary knew as little about Philip as he knew about her, Mary questioned Renard concerning Philip's character and disposition. Holding both of Mary's hands in his, Renard pledged his honor and life that Philip was all she could desire in a husband. But Mary proposed that Philip visit England on his way to the Netherlands, so that she could see him in person before making her final decision.[11]

Charles V would not consider risking the possibility of Mary rejecting Philip after meeting him, so he arranged for Titian's portrait of Philip to be sent to her by its owner, Queen Maria of Hungary. Maria instructed Renard to inform Mary that Philip's portrait must be studied at a distance in order to perceive the likeness.[12] After viewing Philip's portrait, Mary assured Renard that she would accept the young prince.[13]

Quietly at work amidst the excitement of the marriage negotiations in England was the painter from Utrecht, Antonio Moro. Moro's early portrait of the queen's financial wizard, Sir Thomas

Gresham, in a suit of informal clothing usually worn only at home during leisure hours is striking proof of Moro's artistic activity outside the imperial chambers.

Dressed in a white doublet under a carefully buttoned yellow vest, the thirty-year-old Gresham stands with both hands grasping an Oriental cloth-covering on the bannister. The portrait exhibits the basic characteristics of Moro's style: thoroughness, conscientiousness, and faithfulness to external appearances. The head is emphasized by the light falling on the viewer's side of the model's face. Forehead, temple, cheek, and ear project forward. Gresham's gaze, angular to the turn of the head, is directed past the viewer. The skin is fully detailed. Composure and stature underscore the individuality expressed in his face. The portrait, showing a tense and decisive Gresham, is convincing evidence of Antonio Moro's superior craftsmanship. His special blend of realism and spiritual significance. of diligent description and dignified gesture, was not equalled by any of his contemporaries, not even by Titian.

While in England Moro painted portraits of Sir Henry Lee Sidney and Lady Sidney, parents of famous Sir Philip Sidney. The artist also produced a portrait of Simon Renard. When in October 29, 1553, Renard wrote triumphantly to Philip that Mary had given him her promise to marry His Highness, Antonio Moro prepared to depart for Utrecht and Metgen.[14]

In 1554 Antonio Moro returned to England, this time aboard an imperial vessel, for Charles V had commissioned him to paint the portrait of Mary Tudor. On June 19, 1554, Philip sent the Marquis of las Navas to England with a magnificent diamond worth eighty thousand crowns for Mary.[15] She proudly wore this diamond on her bridal dress when Moro painted her portrait.

Mary observed the Flemish artist, surely one of the greatest craftsmen of his age, while he prepared the canvas. First, Moro covered the cloth with a flat ground of tempera. Next, he superimposed layer upon layer of semi-transparent oil glazes, which would receive and reflect light. Then, as he placed thin coats of red, blue, or yellow paints on the glazes, she saw the colors become intense as the light seemed to radiate from the interior of the forms. Wherever he overlapped the brilliant pigments, the outlines of Mary's face, hands, clothing, and jewelry softened while the tones fused and blended. On her face and arms he applied several layers of flesh tone paint.

The overall effect was one of extraordinary richness of color. The entire canvas appeared bathed in an atmospheric luster. His success was reflected in Mary's joy at seeing her likeness. He employed his magic of colorization, painting Mary's portrait in the most extravagant coloristic manner possible. Capturing the proud bearing of the slight-figured woman and the firm gaze of her piercing gray eyes, he penetrated beyond the external dignity expressed in the portrait. Moro's realism portrayed her as a mature Queen of England. The portrait reflects not only Mary's intrinsic beauty and infirmities but also her innate goodness, her joyless adolescence, her powerful will, and the great personal courage which enabled her to face adversity and rebellion. The queen holds a red rose in her hand. The realism with which Antonio Moro had executed the portraits of royalty in the past, and on which the artist's fame was based, was nowhere more effective than in the portrait of Mary Tudor. Its enthusiastic reception raised Moro to an exalted place among European court painters.

The marriage of Philip and Mary was solemnized on the day of St. James, patron saint of Spain. Moro painted both in their wedding costumes. Philip's bridal vestments were provided for him by Mary. His suit was of spotless white satin and gold cloth thickly embroidered with pearls and precious stones. Around his neck Philip wore the collar of the Golden Fleece, the famous Burgundian order, while the brilliant ribbon below his knee served as a badge of the equally illustrious order of the Garter. Mary's dress, also of white satin and gold, was studded and fringed with priceless diamonds. Her bright red slippers and purple velvet overdress or mantle formed a contrast to the rest of her apparel. Around her waist the queen wore a chain of diamonds; around her neck, a string of great pearls barely hidden under a coquettishly protruding collar increased her female charm. Both model and apparel offered the artist unrivalled coloristic possibilities, earning Antonio Moro the honor of being named the worthy successor of the great Holbein.[16]

Moro's fame attracted other Netherlands artists to the English court. Joos van Cleve, a rival of Moro, offered Philip some of his artisitic creations. When he could not win royal favor, the jealous Joos made a scandalous scene in which he called Moro a haughty fool unable to recognize a master in front of his very eyes. He also slandered Metgen by recommending that Moro return to Utrecht to protect her from the canons of Utrecht. When Moro assumed a threatening attitude, Joos crawled under a table to hide. Moro then left the painter's company, considering it beneath his dignity to associate further with Joos van Cleve.[17]

The grateful Queen Mary showered Moro with golden chains and a yearly pension of one hundred pounds sterling. Her portrait by Moro was immensely admired by all who saw it, and when Moro left England with Philip in August of 1555, he brought a copy of it to Charles V. The emperor accepted the portrait but failed to remunerate Moro for it. The astute Granvelle came to the artist's aid. During a visist to Charles V, Granvelle stopped to view the portrait; praising the beauty of Mary and the artistry of Moro, he asked Charles how much money he had given Moro for such a magnificent painting. Surprised, the emperor replied that he had given nothing for it, but inquired of the bishop what remuneration would be suitable. Granvelle advised Charles that so beautiful a portrait was worth at least a thousand gilders or three hundred ducats, whereupon the emperor charged Granvelle to settle the matter with the artist.[18]

Prior to his final departure from England, Antonio Moro painted many miniatures on wood as gifts to English courtiers and members of the Order of the Golden Fleece.[19] Some art historians allege that Moro visited England once more in 1568, but this assertion must be disputed. The evidence for his visit consists solely of a portrait of an aging Sir Thomas Gresham, dated in 1568. But in 1568 Gresham, known as the "Queen's merchant," left Antwerp where he had been residing for some time. Moro, who was also living in Antwerp as a member of the painter's guild of St. Lukas, completed Gresham's portrait prior to his departure.[20]

Without question, Antonio Moro's effort at Mary Tudor's court represents one of the greatest artistic achievements of the century. His paintings of Mary Tudor would have sufficed alone to establish him among the greatest portrait painters of the sixteeth or any century. Following Moro's triumph in England, Philip II invited him to become the first official Spanish court painter, for there was, as yet, no tradition of Spanish court portraiture.[21] The result was the development of the first purely secular painting in the history of Spanish art. As a court portraitist, Antonio Moro's development was one of subtle growth and change. Early in his career he utilized as a compositional scheme the standing pose next to a table or a chair, and he adhered to this technique thereafter. Over the years, however, Moro's brush strokes grew broader, with the result that his models appeared more natural and relaxed; a side effect was the sense of a freer circulation of air around his sitters amidst other elements in the paintings.

The Spanish court portrait was, indeed, Antonio Moro's creation. Alonso Sánchez Coello, Moro's student, and Pantoja de la Cruz, Sánchez Coello's disciple, both followed Moro's pattern and employed his techniques, portraying royal personalities inside their chambers or before the costly mirrors of the court. A similar neutral sphere is still present in Veláquez' early court portraits. Later and under the influence of the Venetian school, Veláquez took the court portrait outdoors, using the broad landscape in the background to emphasize the dignity of the models while also freeing the portrait from a narrow courtly atmosphere.[22] Without doubt, the Veláquez portrait of Innocent X seated in his armchair was influenced by Moro's portrait of Mary Tudor, and his portait of the buffoon Antonio el Tugles, now in the Prado, was inspired by Moro's portrait of Granvelle's buffoon, now in the Louvre.

Most of Moro's later life was spent in the Low Countries, except for a short sojourn in Spain in 1559. He died in Antwerp some time between April 17, 1576[23], and November 4, 1576[24]. Since the artist was fifty-six years old at the time of his death, his birth can be fixed in the year 1519. A notorial protocol in the Utrecht cathedral on May 12, 1577, cites Antonio Moro's "blessed memory."[25]

After Moro's death a new generation, not a student of his among them — Adriaen T. Key, Frans Pourbus, and Frans Floris are choice representatives — captured the field that once belonged to Moro. Although they had not studied under him, they found it prudent to copy Moro's style so closely that much of their work showed that they were, indirectly, at least, his disciples.[26]

These younger artists also followed Moro's lead in choosing portraiture when the division of painting into genres and the specialization of painters into portraiture, historical works, and landscapes occurred in the sixteenth century.[27] Antonio Moro's legacy of psychological portrait studies laid the groundwork for the development of the north Netherland portrait schools of Haarlem and Amsterdam. Even though Moro's direct influence on portrait painters was limited to the sixteenth century, his work was timeless, and he is as much admired today by those who know his work as he was by his contemporaries.

Notes

1. Some helpful works on the life of Antonio Moro are Henri Hyman, *Antonio Moro, son oevre et son temps* (Bruxelles: G. Van Oest & Cie., 1910); George Marlier, *Anthonis Mor van Dashorst* (Bruxelles: Palais de Academies, 1934); and F. Schmidt-Degener, *Antonio Moro* (Jaarsverslag Vereeniging Rembrandt, 1930).
2. L. C. J. Frerichs, *Antonio Moro* (Amsterdam: Utgave Van H. I. W. Becht, 1947), p. 3.
3. Carel van Mander, *Dutch and Flemish Painters* (New York: Arno Press, 1969), pp. 142-143, 430-431.
4. Gert von der Osten and Horst Vey, *Painting and Sculpture in Germany and the Netherlands 1500-1600* (Baltimore: Penguin Books, 1969), pp. 181-184. See also Carel van Mander, *Schilderboek* (Haarlem: Paschier van Westbusch, 1604), p. 142.
5. Margrit Jay, *Antonio Moro: Royal Court Painter, 1519-1576* (unpublished Ph.D. dissertation, Texas Christian University, 1975), p. 11, n. 16.
6. Frerichs, *Antonio Moro*, p. 3.
7. Von der Osten and Vey, *Painting and Sculpture in Germany and the Netherlands 1500-1600*, pp. 182-183.
8. Max J. Friedländer, *Landscape, Portrait, Still-Life, Their Origin and*

Development (New York: Philosophical Library, 1950), p. 132.

9. *The Praeger Encyclopedia of Old Masters*, Joachim Fernan, ed. (New York: Frederick A. Praeger, 1959), p. 215.
10. Valerian Von Loga, *Anthonis Mor als Hofmaler Karl V und Philipp II* (Wien: Tempsky, 1908), p. 103.
11. Great Britain Public Records Office, Belgian Transcripts, Vol. i, 497-505.
12. Letter of Maria of Hungary to Simon Renard, dated Nov. 19, 1553, in Charles Weiss, ed., *Papiers d'Etat du Cardinal Granvelle* (Paris: Imprimerie Royale, 1843), IV, 145.
13. J. M. Stone, *Mary I, Queen of England* (London: Sands & Co., 1901), pp. 265-266; see also letter of Simon Renard to the Emperor Charles V, dated October 31, 1553, in Great Britain Public Records Office, Belgian Transcripts, Vol. i, 600-602.
14. Max J. Friedländer, *Die altniederländische Malerei* (Leyden, 1936), Vol. XIII, p. 126. See also Jay, *Antonio Moro: Royal Court Painter*, p. 46
15. Prudencio de Sandoval, *Historia de la vida y hechos del emperador Carlos V* (Pamplona: Diego Rodriguez, 1614), p. 761.
16. Frerichs, *Antonio Moro*, p. 38.
17. Van Mander, *Dutch and Flemish Painters*, p. 107.
18. *Ibid.*, p. 143.
19. Von Loga, *Anthonis Mor*, p. 105.
20. Walsh, *Philip II*, pp. 50, 298; see also Jay, *Antonio Moro: Royal Court Painter*, pp. 94-98.
21. Harold Osborn, ed., *The Oxford Campanion to Art* (Oxford: Clarendon Press, 1970), pp. 1083-1084.
22. Frerichs, *Antonio Moro*, p. 58.
23. Christian Kramm, *De Levens en Werken der Hollandsche en Vlaamsche Kunstchilders* (Amsterdam, 1860), Vol. 4, 1162-1163. See also Appendix, n. 1.
24. A. Buchelius, "Res Pictoriae" uitgegeven en toegelicht door Dr. G. J. Hoogewerft en J. Q. van Regteren (Altena). *Quellenstudien zur Jolländischen Kunstgeschichte* (Gravenhage: Hoogewerfte en Regteren, 1928).
25. A. Bredius, "Wanners stierf Antonie Mor van Dashorst?" in *Oud-Holland*, 1918, p. 175.
26. Frerichs, *Antonio Moro*, p. 58.
27. Von der Osten and Vey, *Painting and Sculpture in Germany and the Netherlands 1500-1600*, p. 288.

3

Cromwell and the "Slaughtered Saints" of Piedmont*

by
Thomas Auffenberg
Ouachita Baptist University

"Avenge O Lord thy slaughter'd Saints, whose bones
Lie scatter'd on the Alpine mountains cold."
John Milton, *On the late Massacher in Piedmont* (1655)

Oliver Cromwell's zealous commitment to Protestantism constitutes a vital key to understanding his career and personality. His vigorous participation in the Civil War, his ruthless suppression of the Irish rebels, and his domestic policies as Lord Protector all bear the stamp of his strong religious convictions. Certainly, this dedication also influenced his foreign policy, although the extent to which it dictated his actions remains the subject of debate.[1]

After the conclusion of peace with Holland in April, 1654, the Lord Protector's devotion to the so-called "Protestant Interest" became an extremely influential facet of his foreign policy.[2] The Puritan leader sincerely hoped to unite his European co-religionists under England's leadership, and he therefore held an abiding interest in their fate. In pursuit of this ideal, it was only natural for Cromwell to work for peace among Protestant nations and support the cause of endangered dissenters on the Continent.

Nevertheless, it would be a mistake to assume that Cromwell was motivated solely by pious convictions in the formulation of his foreign policy. The Protector personally saw no inherent conflict between religious and national policies, declaring in a speech before a parliamentary delegation in 1657 that, "if any one

*Research on this topic was made possible by a Woodrow Wilson Dissertation Fellowship for 1972-1973 and a faculty research grant from Ouachita Baptist University for 1974-1975.

whatsoever think the Interest of Christians and the Interest of the Nation inconsistent, I wish my soul may never enter into his or their secrets!"[3] Although Cromwell's foreign policy was in many respects "purely nationalistic,"[4] it also reflected a deeply ecumenical concern for the sufferings of co-religionists, and he proved himself willing to intervene on their behalf wherever possible. This dedication for the cause abroad was amply reflected in the Lord Protector's zealous activities on behalf of the persecuted Protestants of Piedmont. Not only did he intercede for them on the diplomatic front, but he also organized and supervised a major collection in England for their benefit.

The Piedmont Protestants, also known as Vaudois and Waldensians, lived in the mountainous Alpine valleys bordering France, but were under the suzerainty of the Duke of Savoy. They were spiritual descendants of the twelfth-century heretic Peter Waldo, and as such were regarded in the sixteenth and seventeenth centuries as primitive Protestants who had anticipated the Reformation. By Cromwell's time the Waldensians had embraced many of the doctrines of John Calvin. Long the victims of periodic persecution, they had enjoyed a certain degree of religious liberty since the mid-sixteenth century, although this toleration existed only within certain well defined geographical limits. By the 1650's, however, the Vaudois had expanded far beyond their original borders. Duke Charles Emmanuel II and Andreas Galstaldus, Conservator General of the Catholic faith in Piedmont, were anxious to reverse this trend and secure the conversion of the dissenters where possible. Catholic priests began entering the Vaudois communities for this purpose, which inevitably led to trouble. Rumors reached the ducal court at Turin that the Protestants had murdered a priest and skinned other Catholic missionaries alive. Although the authenticity of these reports was dubious, they provided the duke with the pretext needed for publication of a harsh decree. On January 25, 1655, he ordered all Protestants in the Vaudois to leave their homes within three days and return to one of the four territories higher in the Alps originally assigned to them. The edict gave those remaining behind twenty days to embrace Catholicism; those who refused faced confiscation of all their property and even the threat of execution.[5]

The duke's decree naturally caused panic among the Vaudois, but it did not result in a general compliance. Instead, the inhabitants of the region vainly attempted to secure an amelioration of its provisions. In February, John Pell, Cromwell's representative to the Swiss cantons, reported to Secretary of State John Thurloe that the Piedmontese dissenters were secretly looking to the Lord Protector for help, but dared not petition him openly for fear of giving the duke a pretext for branding them as traitors.[6]

On April 16 the duke's army, augmented by some French and Irish expatriate troops, launched a general attack against the Vaudois settlements. The Marquis of Pianezza, the Catholic commander, evidently resorted to treachery to complete the conquest. He promised the Protestants a full pardon if they would consent to the quartering of three regiments among them as a sign of their loyalty to their prince. The inhabitants agreed, only to be subjected to a violent massacre on April 24. The avenging army publicly hanged many leading elders of the Protestant church and murdered numerous women and children during a brief period of indiscriminate slaughter. Following the initial bloodletting, the Marquis ordered all survivors to leave their homes within twenty-four hours or else immediately convert to the Church of Rome. Most fled to higher regions in the mountains, where many subsequently perished from exposure and deprivation. Contemporary reports estimated the dead at 6000 and the displaced at 16,000.[7]

News of the atrocities, embellished with exaggerated details, soon reached Puritan England. Shocking reports circulated that soldiers at Tailleret had decapitated 150 women and children and had subsequently boiled the heads and eaten the brains of their victims. Furthermore, Englishmen heard that Catholics had cut out the hearts of some Protestants while the unfortunates were still alive and had poured powder into the wounds of other martyrs, then set them on fire.[8] Lorenzo Paulucci, the Venetian Secretary in England, reported to his counterpart in Paris that Cromwell heard the details of the massacre with tears in his eyes.[9] He also informed his Venetian superiors of rumors that Cromwell was considering the use of the English fleet in the Mediterranean for retaliatory raids against Savoy and that he planned to transport the Piedmont refugees to new homes in Ireland.[10] In a letter of

May 8, 1655, to Pell, Thurloe wrote that the Protector had taken the matter "very much to heart" and expressed his opinion that the use of French troops in the attack would probably delay the proposed treaty with France.[11] William Nieuport, the Dutch ambassador, wrote that the Puritan leader "was astonished to the utmost" by the Piedmont atrocities and was "ready to venture his all for the protection of the Protestant religion . . . ."[12]

Cromwell was indeed outraged by the Duke of Savoy's actions, and he devoted much time during the next few months to diplomatic activity aimed at restoring the Vaudois to their former privileges and homes. On May 25 he sent letters to the duke as well as several other European sovereigns concerning the massacre. In his epistle to Duke Charles, Cromwell said that he had received the news about the Vaudois "with extream Grief and Compassion;" and he begged the duke to revoke the January edict and compensate the refugees for their losses. The Lord Protector vowed that he felt it was his "Duty to God" to do everything in his power to "relieve and succour" the Waldensians.[13]

Cromwell urged young King Louis XIV to intercede for the Vaudois, reminding him of the benevolent treatment accorded to French Protestants by his grandfather, Henry IV. In another letter sent to Cardinal Mazarin, the Protector pleaded with the prelate to intervene on behalf of the "harmless and indigent" victims of persecution. He reminded Mazarin that one of the main reasons England was contemplating an alliance with France was because Protestants enjoyed certain guaranteed rights in the realm.[14]

Other letters went to the kings of Sweden and Denmark, the Prince of Transylvania, the United Provinces, and the evangelical cities of Switzerland. In all these epistles Cromwell stressed the threat the Catholic attack in the Vaudois represented for the rest of Protestant Europe, and he called upon his fellow rulers to join him in a crusade against Savoy should the duke prove intransigent. He asked his fellow heads of state to write the duke to plead the case of the persecuted Vaudois.[15] All of these pleas reflected the Protector's strong vision of a common Protestant cause.

English foreign policy in 1655 was at a crossroads, with both Spain and France eager for a military alliance with the English government. An alliance with France provided certain obvious advantages, including the expulsion of Charles II from Louis XIV's court and the consequent elimination of the threat of a royalist invasion supported by French arms.[16] Even though France was potentially both a more dangerous enemy and a more powerful ally than Spain, Cromwell steadfastly refused to sign an accord with the French so long as the Vaudois question remained unsettled. He was determined to use the promise of an alliance as an inducement for the French to pressure the Duke of Savoy into making concessions.

Cromwell appointed Samuel Morland, a young assistant to Secretary Thurloe, as his special representative concerning the Piedmont affair. Morland left London on May 26, carrying letters to the French king and Duke of Savoy. He met with Louis and Mazarin at La Fère on June 1, forwarding from there the young monarch's pledge assuring Cromwell that he had not sanctioned the use of French troops in the massacre and promising to do all he could to help the Vaudois. Morland then proceeded to the court of Savoy, arriving on June 24. The youthful emissary made a bold speech in Latin before the duke and his mother, comparing the massacre of the Waldensians to Nero's cruelest persecutions. The duke and his ministers unsuccessfully tried to convince Morland that rumors of the atrocities had been greatly exaggerated. Failing to secure the repeal of the January edict, Cromwell's envoy left Piedmont in mid-July and went to Geneva to await developments.[17]

Meanwhile, the Protector was still refusing to ratify the treaty with France, insisting that the agreement contain a clause repudiating any French aid for use against the Piedmont dissenters.[18] The French insisted that they could only entreat — not command — the duke.[19] Dissatisfied with apparent French intransigence, Cromwell in late July sent George Downing as a second envoy to the court of Savoy, but this proved unnecessary.[20]

Mazarin, eager to reach an early agreement with the English, instructed the French ambassador at Turin to insist upon an immediate settlement of the Vaudois question. The result was the Treaty of Pignerol, signed August 19, 1655. The agreement substantially revoked the January edict, slightly enlarged the original area of toleration, and allowed more time for Protestants remaining within Catholic territories to dispose of their property before moving. Cromwell was not completely satisfied with the treaty, feeling that it was "destructive" to the interest of the Vaudois.[21] Nevertheless, the Lord Protector's diplomatic intervention had been instrumental both in securing the Waldensians the right to return to their homeland and in reaffirming most of their traditional liberties.

In addition to his diplomatic activities, Cromwell also sponsored a massive collection throughout England and Ireland for the Piedmontese. Swiss cities, such as Geneva and Zurich, as well as the Dutch, had conducted collections for the Vaudois within weeks after the events of April.[22] Prominent Puritans throughout England called for a similar endeavor. On May 17, the elders of several London churches petitioned the Lord Protector to help the "precious remnant" preserved from the fury of the Catholic army.[23] After considering the Piedmont situation in the Council, Cromwell decided to sponsor financial relief for the refugees in the form of a charity brief. Briefs were governmental letters patent authorizing collections in the nation's churches for specified purposes, most commonly to compensate the victims of costly fires and to help repair damaged parish churches.[24] On a few occasions during the reigns of Elizabeth I and her immediate Stuart successors, however, briefs had been used to raise money for persecuted Continental Protestants.[25]

On May 25 Cromwell issued a proclamation setting aside June 14 as a solemn day of fasting and humiliation in memory of the massacred Waldensians. The directive urged congregations to contribute liberally to the general collection scheduled on the same day.[26] On June 1 the government published instructions governing the collection of the brief. Rather than relying solely upon donations gathered during the church service on the appointed day, ministers and churchwardens were empowered to solicit contributions door to door throughout their parishes. Within twenty days the church officers would turn the money over to the local mayor or nearest justice of the peace for forwarding to Mayor Christopher Pack and Alderman Thomas Vyner, the London Officials designated as general treasurers of the Vaudois fund. Cromwell also appointed a committee of nine trusted advisers to supervise the general operation and the distribution of donations among the needy.[27]

Shortly after issuing these instructions, the government extended the collection to Ireland. The Protector received a letter from forty-five officers stationed there expressing their deep concern over the fate of the Vaudois and urging him to take vigorous action. The officers even suggested that God had exalted Cromwell primarily for the purpose of aiding distressed Protestants.[28] On June 15 the Lord Deputy and his Council set aside July 5 as a general collection day in Ireland for the Piedmont brief. Cromwell's original declaration was reprinted for distribution throughout the island. All Irish contributions were ultimately received by the mayor of Dublin and two of his aldermen, who forwarded the contributions to the authorities in London.[29]

The Vaudois brief evoked widespread participation throughout the Puritan realm. Even ships of the fleet anchored at Lyme held special services to collect money for the persecuted Waldensians.[30] Local preachers assailed their congregations in sermons filled with righteous indignation over the atrocities committed in Savoy. Worshippers on their way to divine service discovered many local churches painted red to remind parishioners of the nature of the bloodbath inflicted upon their fellow Protestants. Cromwell personally pledged £2000 to the brief.[31] Common tradesmen in London, who normally gave only a few pence to briefs, reportedly contributed £10 or £20 each to the Vaudois collection.[32] The commissioners were so thorough in the door to door solicitations that they even visited the houses of ambassadors or other foreign dignitaries.[33] It soon became evident that the brief would produce an enormous amount of money. "The certain sum which hath been gathered is not yet known," the French ambassador reported on June 21, "but must needs amount to a vast sum; for every body gave something to seem charitable, and the ministers have plaid their parts to some purpose, to stir up the people to assist their persecuted brethren."[34]

Despite the widespread participation in the benevolence, the Council discovered that the brief had not been observed in all the nation's parishes. Consequently, on July 12 Cromwell issued another proclamation. He ordered all parishes that had not yet participated in the collection to do so as soon as possible, and any outstanding contributions were to be sent to London immediately.[35] Six months later the Council, still concerned about delinquent parishes, sent new letters to the justices of the peace ordering them to collect and forward tardy donations to the capital.[36]

Rumors circulated among the ambassadors in London about the amount raised by the Vaudois brief and the purposes for which the fund would be employed. Both Paulucci and Nieuport estimated in July that the collection had already raised approximately £100,000. The former speculated that most of this money would be spent on the English navy after a respectable sum had been sent overseas.[37] Royalists exiled on the Continent also expressed deep fears about Cromwell's plans for the brief money. Secretary Edward Nicholas wrote his friend Joseph Jane in September that he was afraid the Protector intended to use the fund to hire a Swiss bodyguard.[38] To the Lord Protector's credit, all of these rumors were without foundation.

The elaborate account book for the 1655 Vaudois brief, prepared by treasurers Pack and Vyner in November, 1657, lists total contributions of £38,907 7s. 3d., an amount surpassed by only two other seventeenth-century briefs.[39] This sum included the £2000 gift from Cromwell, as well as over £200 given by servants and officials of the Protector's household. Ireland raised almost £1100 for the brief, but the bulk of the contributions came from English parishes. An impressively high number of the nation's parishes contributed to the brief, 8,636 out of approximately 10,000. The citizens of London and Westminster donated nearly one-fourth of the final total, with twenty-nine of the capital's parishes raising over £100 each. Donations in the countryside naturally tended to be smaller, with few parishes collecting more than £10 and most averaging about £1. Nevertheless, seven English counties in addition to Middlesex collected over £1000 each.[40]

In order to insure equitable and rapid distribution among the needy, Cromwell appointed Morland and Pell to oversee the transfer of funds from England to the Vaudois. The first money to reach the refugees was the £2000 personal contribution from the Lord Protector, sent in thirty-four installments between May and September, 1655.[41] The Vaudois badly needed assistance. In

October, Pell reported to Secretary Thurloe that they were in a pitiful condition, "needing all things, having nothing fit for men." Unless additional aid arrived soon, he warned, many would perish from lack of proper food, clothing, and shelter.[42]

Cromwell retained a deep interest in the distribution of the brief money. In November, 1655, Secretary Thurloe wrote Pell that the Protector expected to be informed about the allocation of the money and wanted it to go to those in greatest need. Cromwell also requested information on how his original £2000 gift had been utilized.[43] In February, 1656, the commissioners reported on how the £9500 so far received by the Vaudois had been distributed.[44]

	£	s.	d.
Initially spent for maintaining soldiers, buying ammunition, and other needs	1913	5	0
For covers and bedding	107	1	9
For linen, shirts, goods for sick	72	16	9
For corn for bread and seed	2340	0	0
For 2700 ells of cloth and 640 pairs shoes	450	15	0
For feed-corn and more urgent needs	4000	2	0
To physicians for medicine	39	0	0
Remaining in their hands	90	12	6
	9013	13	0
Bad money or lost in transit	486	7	0
Total	9500	0	0

Pell having returned to his duties in Zurich, Morland remained in Geneva for a year to oversee the continued transfer of funds to the Vaudois. He gradually developed a list of principles governing the distribution of the donations. Rather than providing proportional compensation to all who had suffered losses, the money first went to those in greatest need, as the Protector had suggested.[45] The young envoy returned to England late in 1656 and prepared a general account of his expeditures. On January 29, 1657, he wrote his former colleague Pell that the Council had approved his book of accounts as "exact, perfect, and satisfactory," concluding, "I bless God I am come off with honour."[46]

Almost £22,000 had reached the Piedmont Protestants by the end of 1657, and before Cromwell's death the Council of State allocated an additional £3000 of the fund to be used for whatever purposes the Waldensians felt necessary.[47] Another £1254 went to provide annuities for certain ministers, military men, physicians, schoolmasters, and students; while an additional £500 was given to twenty Bohemian families who were also the victims of religious persecution.[48] Unfortunately, some of the money never reached the valleys, for at least £6700 was diverted to other purposes during the summer of 1659 by the republican government which replaced Richard Cromwell.[49] Nevertheless, the overwhelming majority of the contributions did reach the Piedmontese and provided invaluable asssistance to the sufferers.

Cromwell maintained an active interest in the fate of the Vaudois Protestants until his death in September, 1658. His instructions to William Lockhart, his new ambassador to France, in April, 1656, urged the emissary to discuss the "miserable condition" of the Piedmontese with Louis XIV and Mazarin at the earliest opportunity.[50] Less than four months before his death the Protector wrote a personal letter to the French monarch renewing his complaints about the harsh terms of the Treaty of Pignerol and objecting to alleged violations of the agreement. Cromwell was especially indignant about rumors of renewed attempts to interfere with the religious liberty of the Vaudois. The Puritan leader even seriously considered a scheme for transferring the valleys to the sovereignty of the French king in the hopes that this would provide the Waldensians with more secure toleration.[51]

The diplomatic and philanthropic aid for the Vaudois which Cromwell so vigorously championed provides useful clues toward the understanding his personality and his foreign policy. His actions clearly reflect his determination to pursue a policy in line with the "two greatest Concernments that God hath in the world" — religion and national interest.[52] His activities on behalf of the Piedmont Protestants obviously were not undertaken solely for narrow nationalistic purposes. In comparison with the Low Countries, Ireland, and even the Baltic, Piedmont had little strategic or economic importance for England. Cromwell's strong religious convictions and his image of himself as the leader and defender of Protestants provided him with all the motivations he needed to interfere in the internal affairs of a foreign country. Nor was the Piedmont intervention an isolated example of the Protector's attitudes, for in 1658 he authorized a collection throughout his realm for the benefit of persecuted Polish Protestants.[53] It raised over £10,000.[54]

Cromwell's work on behalf of the suffering Waldensians was not limited to raising money on their behalf. He skillfully utilized the precarious diplomatic situation of the mid-1650's to win important concessions for the Piedmontese. By delaying the signing of an accord with France until the plight of the Vaudois was remedied, the Protector provided Cardinal Mazarin with strong reasons for applying pressure on the Duke of Savoy to abandon his blatant policies of persecution. The resultant Treaty of Pignerol paved the way for a formal alliance between the French and English a few months later.[55]

The ardent zeal with which Cromwell approached the Piedmontese situation may seem curiously anachronistic in the more secular atmosphere of the twentieth century. His attitude certainly seems hypocritical considering his own forced transportation of thousands of Catholic dissenters in Ireland. Yet Cromwell, convinced of the righteousness of his cause, saw no such inconsistency; and his intervention on behalf of the Waldensians was a popular action among his fellow countrymen. This is amply demonstrated by the generous response of the nation to the 1655 collection. The whole episode underlines the impossibility of divorcing religious convictions from public policies in Puritan England. In Cromwell's mind the welfare of the English nation was irrevocably tied to the fate of European Protestantism. He consequently saw his tireless work on behalf of the afflicted Piedmontese as fulfilling a dual purpose: service to England and service to God.

Notes

1. For a brief summary of recent interpretations of the role religion played in determining Cromwell's foreign policy, see Michael Roberts, "Cromwell and the Baltic," in *Essays in Swedish History* (London: Weidenfeld and Nicolson, 1967), pp. 138-143. Also consult Robert S. Paul, *The Lord Protector: Religion and Politics in the Life of Oliver Cromwell* (London: Lutterworth Press, 1955), pp. 339-342; and Menna Prestwich, "Diplomacy and Trade in the Protectorate," *The Journal of Modern History*, XXII (1950), 103-104, 120-121.
2. C. H. Firth asserted that one of the three major features of Cromwell's foreign policy was a "desire to maintain and spread the Protestant religion." C. H. Firth, *Oliver Cromwell and the Rule of the Puritans in England* (London: G. P. Putnam's Sons, 1900), p. 370.
3. Wilbur Cortez Abbott, ed., *The Writings and Speeches of Oliver Cromwell* (4 vols.; London: Oxford University Press, 1937-1947), IV, 445.
4. Christopher Hill, "The English Revolution and the Brotherhood of Man," in *Puritanism and Revolution* (New York: Shocken Books, 1958), p. 125.
5. Thomas Birch, ed., *A collection of the State Papers of John Thurloe* (7 vols.; London: Thomas Woodward, 1742), III, 476-477 [hereafter cited as *Thurloe Papers*]; A Short and Faithful Account of the late commotions in the valleys of Piedmont (London: for W. E. and G. L., 1655), pp. 1-13; *A collection of the several papers sent to his Highness the Lord Protector* (London: H. Robinson, 1655), pp. 1-3; S. R. Gardiner, *History of the Commonwealth and Protectorate* (4 vols.; London: Longmans, Green, and Co., 1913-1916), IV, 178-181.
6. Robert Vaughan, ed., *The Protectorate of Oliver Cromwell and the State of Europe during the Early Part of the Reign of Louis XIV* (2 vols.; London: Henry Colburn, 1839), I, 139-140.
7. *A collection of several papers*, pp. 23-25. Although the reports were undoubtedly exaggerated, at least 300 — perhaps many more — Vaudois had been killed. Abbott, *Writings and Speeches*, III, 707; David Masson, *The Life of John Milton* (reprint ed.; 7 vols.; New York: Peter Smith, 1946), V, 39-40. See also Gardiner, *History*, IV, 181-185.
8. *Thurloe Papers*, III, 412-413. See also *Thurloe Papers*, III, 411, 441, and *Mercurius Politicus*, May 10, 1655.
9. Great Britian, Public Record Office, *Calendar of State Papers and Manuscripts Relating to English Affairs, Existing in the Archives and*

Collections of Venice, and in Other Libraries of Northern Italy (23 vols.; London: H. M. Stationery Office, 1911-1947), XXX, 66. [hereafter cited as *CSPV*]

10. Vaughan, *Protectorate*, I, 174-176.
11. *CSPV*, XXX, 63. Abbott asserts that the Vaudois persecution added support to the idea of transplanting the Irish to Connaught and replacing them with Protestants from Britain. Abbott, *Writings and Speeches*, III, 521.
12. *Thurloe Papers*, III, 476-477.
13. Abbott, *Writings and Speeches*, III, 724-725. This letter and the other epistles to European leaders concerning the massacre were probably drafted by John Milton. Masson, *Milton*, V, 40.
14. Abbott, *Writings and Speeches*, III, 726-727.
15. Ibid., 726-732.
16. For a summary of motivations behind a French alliance, see Roger Crabtree, "The Idea of a Protestant Foreign Policy," in Ivan Roots, ed., *Cromwell: A Profile* (New York: Hill and Wang, 1973), pp. 179-184. See also Firth, *Cromwell*, pp. 375-376.
17. Masson, *Milton*, V, 42-43.
18. Vaughan, *Protectorate*, I, 219.
19. *Thurloe Papers*, III, 617.
20. The Protector's letter is printed in Abbott, *Writings and Speeches*, III, 788-789. In addition, Cromwell urged the French king to punish severely French officers who had participated in the massacre.
21. Abbott, *Writings and Speeches*, III, 818-819; Gardiner, *History*, IV, 187-191.
22. *CSPV*, XXX, 76-77; Vaughan, *Protectorate*, I, 174; George F. Warner, ed., *The Nicholas Papers* (4 vols.; London: The Camden Society, 1886-1920), II, 331.
23. Great Britain, Public Record Office, State Papers, Domestic, Interregnum, 97, No. 44. [hereafter cited as SP 18/] Other abbreviations of State Papers employed in this paper include SP 16/ for State Papers, Domestic, Charles I; SP 25/ for State Papers, Council of State; and SP 45/ for State Papers, Various.
24. The standard work on briefs, though outdated, is W. A. Bewes, *Church Briefs* (London: A. and G. Black, 1896). See also Thomas L. Auffenberg, "Organized English Benevolence: Charity Briefs, 1625-1705" (Ph.D. dissertation, Vanderbilt University, 1973).
25. James I approved a brief for the inhabitants of Geneva, then threatened by the Duke of Savoy. See Bewes, *Church Briefs*, pp. 93-95; Charles I sponsored three collections for Protestant ministers exiled from the Palatinate. See SP 16/91, No. 71; SP 45/10, No. 117; SP 16/286, No. 56.

26. SP 18/97, No. 82. The declaration is also printed in Bewes, *Church Briefs*, pp. 149-150.
27. *Instructions to be observed touching the collection* (London: Henry Hills and John Field, 1655). Also found in SP 18/98, No. 4.
28. *Thurloe Papers*, III, 466-467.
29. *His Highness Declaration Inviting the People of England and Wales to a Day of Humiliation for the Distressed Protestants in Savoy: and the Instructions of his Highness As Also the Order of the Lord Deputy and Council, for Keeping a Day of Humiliation and Collection for their Relief* (Dublin: Henry Hills and John Field, 1655).
30. SP 18/97, Nos. 88-89.
31. *CSPV*, XXX, 72-73.
32. C. H. Firth, ed., *The Clarke Papers* (4 vols.; London: Camden Society, 1891-1901), III, 44.
33. *CSPV*, XXX, 76. Bordeaux, the French ambassador, complained of this zealousness in a letter to his father. *Thurloe Papers*, III, 558.
34. *Thurloe Papers*, III, 568.
35. *A Proclamation for Perfecting the Collection for Relief of the Protestant Inhabitants of the Valleys of Lucern, Angrona, &c* (London: Henry Hills and John Field, 1655).
36. SP 25/76, p. 482, No. 8.
37. *CSPV*, XXX, 87; *Thurloe Papers*, III, 623. Paulucci repeated his suspicions on at least two subsequent occasions. *CSPV*, XXX, 88-89, 93.
38. SP 18/100, No. 84. Jane discounted the idea, writing Nicholas, "Touching Cr's guard, I am not apt to be of opinion that he will adventure to have a guard of strangers, for it must exasperate the army against him, in whom all his trust and strength lyeth . . ." *Nicholas Papers*, III, 47-48. See also letter to Charles II on September 4. SP 18/100, No. 85.
39. *A distinct and Faithful Accompt of All the Receipts, Disbursements, and Remainder of Moneys Collected in England, Wales, and Ireland, for the Relief of the Poor Distressed Protestants in the Valleys of Piemont* [sic] (London: Henry Hills and John Field, 1658), p. 95. [hereafter cited as *Distinct and Faithful Accompt*]
40. Ibid.
41. *Thurloe Papers*, V, 617-620.
42. Vaughan, *Protectorate*, I, 281.
43. Ibid., 286-287.
44. *Thurloe Papers*, V, 621-622.
45. Morland's general principles are printed in *Thurloe Papers*, V, 640-644, and *Distinct and Faithful Accompt*, pp. 103-105.

46. Vaughan, *Protectorate*, II, 102-103. Morland's account is printed in a *Distinct and Faithful Accompt*, pp. 97-112.
47. *Distinct and Faithful Accompt*, p. 111.
48. SP 25/78, pp. 615, 620-622.
49. In the nineteenth century a myth developed that Charles II's government had confiscated the money. For a discussion of this misconception, see William A. Shaw, "The English Government and the Relief of Protestant Refugees," *English Historical Review*, IX (1894), 675-676. Bewes incorrectly blamed Richard Cromwell for the confiscation. Bewes, *Church Briefs*, p. 2. Actually, the confiscated money was utilized for expenses of the English garrison at Dunkirk and the expedition of Major-General John Lambert. Great Britain, Public Record Office, *Calendar of State Papers, Domestic, 1659-1660* (London: H. M. Stationery Office, 1886), pp. 112, 580-583.
50. Abbott, *Writings and Speeches*, IV, 140.
51. Ibid., 811-814.
52. Ibid., 445.
53. *A declaration of His Highness, for a Collection towards the Relief of Divers Protestant Churches driven out of Poland; and of Twenty Protestant Families Driven out of the Confines of Bohemia* (London: Henry Hills and John Field, 1658).
54. Great Britain, Parliament, *Journals of the House of Commons* (London: n.p., n.d.), VIII, 712.
55. Similar views are expressed by Antonia Fraser in her biography, *Cromwell: The Lord Protector* (New York: Alfred A. Knopf, 1973), pp. 540-541. Robert Paul has skillfully pointed out that Cromwell was playing a dangerous game by putting so much pressure on the French, when he was already committed to a war against Spain. Paul, *The Lord Protector*, pp. 338-339.

4

Prison Reforms in the Augustan Age*

by
Ted R. Jamison, Jr.
Southwest Texas State University

By the time of Queen Anne's reign many Englishmen were proud of their country and particularly proud of the constitution. Compared with the absolute monarchies on the continent, England's Bill of Rights stood as a solitary achievement, and whatever oppression remained in England appeared negligible. Yet, the English constitution, a supposed bulwark of human rights, utterly failed in that respect so far as lower class, poverty-stricken people were concerned.

With the 18th century, conditions among the indigent in England had not changed appreciably since the Elizabethan Poor Laws which had been enacted over a century earlier to alleviate their plight. The crime level in the lower strata had, in fact, appallingly increased over the years, and by the time of the accession of George I the prisons and jails of England contained over 500,000 inmates, according to estimates made by John Howard.[1] But the 18th century became the transitional period in social reform after hundreds of years of indifference to the human misery at the lower levels of society. "Out of the complex chemistry of Georgian times," E. N. Williams observed, "the spirit of humanitarianism is the most precious deposit, and it was precipitated by the middle classes."[2] In this era of change, social innovations were numerous, but none more dramatic or important than in the area of legal and prison reform. Many famous men, including Daniel Defoe, Henry Fielding, John Howard, and above all, Bernard Mandeville, became involved in this issue and, in turn, aroused public compassion.

*This essay originally appeared in the August-September 1976 issue of *British History Illustrated*.

Daniel Defoe, one of those in England's middle class who most exposed the miserable conditions of the poor, boldly condemned the injustices and inadequacies in the English legal system. Pointing an accusing finger toward the courts and prisons, he asserted that both institutions encouraged, rather than inhibited, crime. Defoe's outrage was caustically expressed in his famous pamphlet, "The Hymn to the Pillory":

> The first intent of the Laws,
> Was to correct th' Effect, and check the cause;
> And all the ends of Punishment,
> Were only Future Mischiefs to prevent.
> But Justice is inverted when
> Those Engines of the Law,
> Instead of Pinching Vicious Men,
> Keep honest ones in awe;
> To Punish Villains, not to make Men so.[3]

Daniel Defoe learned about the conditions of London prisons firsthand. In 1703 he was given a short term in Newgate, the county prison for Middlesex, for writing the inflammatory pamphlet, "The Shortest Way With the Dissenters." Defoe was forced also to stand three times in the pillory as a result of his criticism of the government.[4] The great Augustan author continued to write vituperative pamphlets throughout the years following his release from Newgate, and in 1713, after producing so-called "Scandalous, Wicked, and Treasonable Libels" in a pamphlet directed against the Hanoverian succession, once again faced the prospect of going to jail. Defoe shuddered at the thought, vividly recalling the horrors of ten years earlier. Fortunately, however, he escaped indictment on the charge.[5]

The prison system in England during Georgian times was an odd mixture of privately owned jails and those operated by local governmental bodies. In any case there was little or no Crown supervision and all the prisons fell into deplorable conditions, unfit for use. In the private jails profits were made from the prisoners' labors as well as from fees paid to the wardens for the necessities of life. Fees were arbitrarily assessed each prisoner for bed, food, clothing, and, when the time came, for discharge from jail. According to the law, the wardens were allowed to keep prisoners incarcerated if any of the Crown-approved fees were not paid. Many times prisoners found innocent in the courts were kept in jails simply because they could not afford to pay the fee required by the warden for release.[6]

After numerous abortive attempts to bring about effective prison reform during the first half of the 18th century, the efforts of one man finally made the country aware of the desperate need for improvement. John Howard, the great philanthropist-humanitarian, single-handedly exposed the intolerable conditions in the English Bridewells.[7] Not only did Howard vividly describe the horrors found in all of England's prisons, which he pesonally visited, but logically proved that the Bridewells were the main contributors to the increase in the crime rate in the 18th century. But Howard's suggested reforms did not become a reality until 1774, and for much of the Georgian period the prisoners suffered in the worst conceivable conditions.[8]

There were, in fact, some mild attempts at reform of the prisons prior to the reign of George III, but little came of them. In 1728 Parliament inquired into the state of the jails (gaols) but passed no legislation.[9] The early Augustan age witnessed the efforts of many humanitarian reformers, but their pleas fell on deaf ears. Certainly Daniel Defoe was deeply concerned about the appalling conditions in England's prisons. He did not, however, persist in instituting the necessary reforms. Defoe focused much of his attention on the plight of England's debtors in *The Review*. As early as 1709 he attacked the absurd practice of imprisoning the unfortunate debtors, who, Defoe lamented, were "in a true literal sense, 'lost men,' given up in death and murdered by inexorable creditors." So often, he said, such prisoners were incarcerated as a result of a personal grudge or revenge and "every unchristian passion" on the part of the creditor.[10] Later in the Hanoverian period when John Howard viewed the futile predicament of the English debtor, he reminded his critics that "a prison pays no debts,"[11] since such prisoners, of course, could rarely meet their obligation while in prison, and there were many reported cases of fifteen years served for a meager sum of thirty or forty shillings. Compounding the plight of the debtor was the practice of imprisoning him with felons. There in the same cell, according to Defoe, they wasted away, were bullied by the hardened criminals, abused by the heartless jailers, and exposed to disease and filth.[12]

Other famous Augustan writers demonstrated concern over the miserable conditions in the English Bridewells. Henry Fielding emphasized the relationship between the increasing crime rate and the disgraceful number of poor throughout the country. Like Defoe, who had remarked about the "swarm of the begging poor" roving throughout England,[13] Fielding accused the middle and upper classes of encouraging and, in fact, directly contributing to the crime rate. Crime, according to Fielding, was precipitated by status-seeking at all levels and each level of society served as the ideal for the next lower. The ostentatious display of wealth by the middle and upper classes only served to encourage robbery.[14]

Fielding, in his *Tom Jones*, subtly accused the corrupt gentry of being the paragon of status-seeking in England. The aspirations and pretentions of Squire Western, his string of hounds and insatiable desire for a marriage alliance for his daughter, illustrated the outrageous behavior of the gentry.[15]

But Fielding's main emphasis on reform stresses the failure of English society to respond adequately to the plight of the poor. The humble and "poor spirited" wound up as beggars, he observed, while those who were bold and clever enough took to stealing.[16] Fielding personally interviewed a highwayman who privately confessed to several robberies. The thief's motives were simple. Debts were owed, and the risk taken to steal money for payments was far less than the gamble that he would be incarcerated for indebtedness.[17] Daniel Defoe agreed with Fielding's view of the debtor's predicament. "The punishing vices in the poor which are daily practiced by the rich," Defoe observed, "seems to me to be setting our constitution with the wrong end upward." Men were made criminals, he continued, "because they want money."[18]

Despite the compassionate words of Defoe and Fielding, there were many of their contemporaries who agreed with the system of throwing debtors into the prisons. John Trenchard, for example, condemned any charity for such men, claiming that it promoted only idleness and laziness. Trenchard viewed the felon and the debtor as one, labeling them as "idle rotting vermin" who were devouring the kingdom and becoming a "publick Nuisance."[19]

Such criticism did not stop the movement for prison reform.

Indeed, new crusaders joined the cause. John Gay wrote *The Beggar's Opera*, a work which was produced for the first time at the Theatre Royal in Lincoln's Inn Fields in 1728.[20] His satirical play gave the theatregoers a vivid picture of lower class London in the early 18th century, for its colorful cast was composed of beggars, prostitutes, pickpockets, pirates, highwaymen, and degenerates. Although the audiences viewed *The Beggar's Opera* as a humorous satire, Gay's work contained an impressive social message, a subliminal sense of tragedy, intermixed with artistic understatements. One of Gay's fictitious robbers, condemned to death at Tyburn, was described by his unusually compassionate jailer:

> He behav'd always well under sentence . . . attended regularly in chapel, sate very quiet, and took good heed both to Prayers and Exhortations. He frequently gave me many blessings for the Prayers, godly exhortations and Advices I gave him; and sometimes he took me by the hand, as I past by him and kiss'd it, particularly that morning he died.[21]

One illustrious member of the opening-night audience at Lincoln's Inn Fields was Gay's close friend, Jonathan Swift. The famous Dean of St. Patrick's praised Gay's boldness and artistic abilities, saying that it would "probably do more good than a thousand sermons."[22]

Among the early humanitarians who argued for prison reform was Bernard Mandeville, the deist author of *Fable of the Bees* (1725) and *An Enquiry into the Causes of the Frequent Executions at Tyburn* (1724). A contemporary of Defoe and Fielding, Mandeville visited many of England's prisons and criticized the upper and middle classes for ignoring the deplorable conditions in the Bridewells. Mandeville not only observed the prisons first hand, but also walked among London's poor and interviewed criminals. Emphasizing the astounding rate of crime in London's streets, Mandeville equated the higher amount of crime with the increase in the ranks of poverty-stricken. The city, he complained, was filled with poor, lazy, and dishonest people who had no hope for improvement.[23]

Bernard Mandeville, appalled by the increased amount of lawlessness in London, was even more outraged by the crimes committeed against the criminals and debtors once they were imprisoned and stood trial. Defoe, in 1704, had charged that many of the justices were drunk during the trials and argued that "every man who is subject to the law, and punishable by it, has a right in the execution of the law upon all offenders equally with himself."[24] Mandeville echoed Defoe's words twenty years later and condemned the common practice of detaining accused persons for months in jails before trial.

Mandeville was especially critical of his own middle class for compounding the felonies of the lower class criminals by purchasing or ransoming their stolen goods from professional criminals. Many upper and middle class victims gladly paid the thief's price for the return of stolen articles, promising not to prosecute. Bernard Mandeville condemned that practice, commonly called "Theftbote," since it only encouraged more crime. In his *Enquiry*, Mandeville reminded his readers that Sir Edward Coke and Sir Matthew Hale had both ruled that "Theftbote" was as serious a felony as the original crime.[25]

Most of all, however, Mandeville centered his criticisms upon the deplorable conditions that he found in the prisons and more particularly the circus-like atmosphere surrounding the frequent hangings at Tyburn, the place of execution for the condemned who were held in Newgate Prison. When he visited Newgate, Mandeville found an average of fifty men, women, and children confined in one dark, stuffy, and filthy cell. The prison itself had virtually no windows for ventilation or light. In 1696 Parliament had passed the Window-tax, which had caused most private prison owners to brick over windows rather than to pay the tax. A prison with twenty windows, by Mandeville's time, would have had to pay an annual tax of only about ten shillings.[26]

Inside the packed cells at Newgate, Mandeville observed an astonishing picture of human misery. As he walked through the corridors he listened to mock trials being conducted in the cells. Experienced criminals instructed the neophytes in cross-examination for the purpose of confusing witnesses. Mandeville visited with several felons who openly boasted of their crimes and were sure that they would be acquitted by the court.[27]

Mandeville made it a special point to visit Newgate on the day appointed for the executions to be held at nearby Tyburn. He was allowed to interview condemned criminals destined for the scaffold and noted that most of them possessed an unnatural coolness in the face of death. With "but one morning to live," he sadly reported, "one would expect a deep sense of sorrow, with all of the signs of a thorough contrition; that either silence or a sober sadness should prevail." But such was not the case with most of the condemned. The scene at Newgate was a nightmare for the sensitive humanitarian, who saw rough turnkeys, angry and hurried, making the necessary preparations for the executions. Some of the condemned, Mandeville noted, were but poor, miserable creatures with "the sharp and dreadful look of Rogues, that beg in chains." There were over two hundred crimes that called for the death penalty by Mandeville's time, and those tragic victims, he said, "would rob you of greater satisfaction."

As he moved through the corridors at Newgate, Mandeville listened to the various noises made by the prisoners. In some cells there was shouting and fighting, and in another there was loud laughter amongst "the seas of Beer that were swill'd; the never-ceasing out cries for more, and the bawling Answers of the Tapsters as continual."[28]

Later in the century, John Howard would express astonishment at the amount of alcoholic beverages consumed by the more affluent prisoners in the Bridewells. To increase profit in the private jails, the owners by law were allowed to sell beer, gin, and ale to the inmates.[29] Mandeville, too, was shocked as he viewed the tremendous volume of alcohol consumed in prison. Approaching each cell with caution, he observed the filthy hands of prisoners reaching through the bars begging for food and water while others stood behind them in a drunken stupor.[30]

Mandeville watched as the Warden of the prison, accompanied by the hangman, entered the cells and moved among the jeering prisoners. The Warden, he observed, attempted to comfort those who were destined to die on that day, but the executioner, "impatient to be gone," swore at the delay. As the condemned were led from their cells, a torrent of people burst through the prison gates. Most were, according to Mandeville, "among the lower rank, and working people, the idlest, and such as are most fond of making Holidays."[31]

The day set aside for executions was always known by the public beforehand. The posted notices were tantamount to an invitation for all pickpockets and thieves to meet at Tyburn. The condemned prisoners were placed in carts and, surrounded by the unruly mob, were transported from the jail to the scaffold. In the Tyburn courtyard, people milled around, playing games, wrestling, drinking, and picking pockets. It was generally a festive mood that prevailed and the crowd yelled and laughed when the condemned were led into the courtyard. Mandeville gave a vivid description of the scene. There, he wrote, stood "an old Sloven, in a wig actually putrified, squeezed up in a corner," offering drinks of gin to passersby. Profane screams and a roar of laughter erupted as someone tossed the carcass of a dead dog into the midst of the mob.

As the condemned were led to the scaffold they were often drunk or near unconsciousness and still drinking huge quantities of gin, carefully fortifying themselves lest "Soberiety [sic] overtake them." When one of the more notorious rogues of the time was being led to death, young criminals, proud of their profession, squeezed through the crowd, crawling between the legs of onlookers and horses to shake hands with their hero. Once the condemned men mounted the scaffold the chaos invariably grew worse and the rugged jailers were forced to beat off the mob with clubs. It was not unusual for people in the crowd to be trampled and killed, for the multitudes on foot were intermixed with elegant carriages and nervous horses.[32]

But the hangman did his job, quickly and dispassionately, with no ceremony. When the body was removed from the noose the mob closed in to watch the surgeons fight over a new subject for their anatomical experiments.[33] Apparently there was a great fear among the condemned prisoners that their bodies might be thus disposed of, a fear that was often greater than death itself. For example, Joseph Blake, a thief nicknamed "Blueskin," made it a condition of his capture that he be buried in a coffin immediately after execution.[34]

The conditions described by Mandeville in 1725 had not changed appreciably fifty years later when John Howard took up the cause of reforms. Debtors and children were still included in the same cells with hardened felons. Perils to health and horrors unknown to most Englishmen still characterized the penal institutions of the land. Prisons were living tombs for their inmates, and many of the accused did not survive their ordeal to stand trial. According to the best estimates, even as late as 1775, disease, starvation, and murders inside the prisons caused the deaths of one in four inmates,[35] and the availability of medical attention to the poor, either in or out of the Bridewells, was negligible.[36]

Inside the jails the scenes of human misery were still appalling and disgraceful. Prisoners could not even stand the smell of their own clothing. John Howard, when visiting a Bridewell, always saturated himself with vinegar to cover up the sickening odor. The food and water portions for each prisoner were meager, to say the least. One or two tiny bits of bread per day along with three pints of stale water for drinking and bathing were provided by the jailers. Often some prisoners located in the lower levels of the dungeons were forgotten by the turnkeys and consequently starved to death. Some prisoners, driven to the point of desperation, ate their straw bedding and the human waste in the cells before expiring. John Howard was shocked to discover that at the Bridewell at Shepton Malet, for example, an average of four persons per week died from starvation and disease.[37]

The most common killer of the inmates was a disease similar to modern typhus, which the English simply called "jail distemper" or "jail fever." Most of the prisons were infected by the disease, which killed off not only the prisoners, but the guards as well. In the Lent Assize in Taunton in 1770, Howard learned that some prisoners infected the entire court, killing the judge, the sergeant, the sheriff, and the jury.[38] And at the one-celled jail at Horsham, he found the prisoners starving and dying and the warden and his wife dead of distemper outside the cell.[39]

The crowded conditions in the dark, unventilated cells were conducive to every conceivable horror. Starving prisoners, weakened from disease, sat chained to the walls awaiting death. Fetters were used on most prisoners, even though by a law passed in the reign of George II they had been declared illegal.[40] There was no medical care for the sick whatsoever, and even the chaplains refused to visit the prisons to comfort those who faced death. The dying, moreover, were usually left alone by their fellow inmates and jailers. When they died, oftentimes their bodies were not removed and were simply left for the vermin to consume.[41] The stronger prisoners persisted in intimidating the weaker, most of whom were unfortunate debtors, and many were forced to strip naked and give their clothes to the bullies. At best the prisoners spent "their time in sloth, profaneness and debauchery."[42]

John Howard, like Bernard Mandeville before him, came to the conclusion that many of England's crimes were actually hatched inside the Bridewells. The professional criminals were allowed frequent visitors who provided them with the money for gin and payoffs to the jailers. "In prison," Howard lamented, "the check of the public eye is removed, and the power of the law is spent."[43]

Some alternatives to prison did exist, however, in the 18th century. The transporting of prisoners to the colonies was a popular practice in the 18th century. Numerous statutes supported such practice and the government encouraged the judges to offer transportation as an option to the guilty. Considerable public money was saved by shipping prisoners out of the country since the government would not have to support their years in prison. The colonial markets usually paid five pounds per head for the criminals and in turn sold them to colonists for ten pounds as cheap labor. Prisoners, of course, could work their way to freedom eventually, and thousands accepted the alternative of transportation rather than face the prospect of prison. During the entire 18th century there was an average of 500 prisoners per year sent by the courts to the colonies. Occasionally, too, some able-bodied prisoners were taken into the army and navy.[44] In a sense, the use of both transportation and military service indicate a growing awareness of the conditions revealed by the early reformers.

The awakening of the humanitarian spirit in the 18th century was not wholly due to the moral questions surrounding the conditions in the prisons. Certainly, John Howard did more than anyone to expose the gigantic economic loss caused by the non-productiveness of the thousands thrown into the Bridewells. Yet, prior to Howard's time, Defoe, Fielding, Gay, Swift, and others had all agreed that reform was needed. Their efforts lacked cohesiveness and they failed to provide clear social or economic programs for the government. Mandeville in particular seriously attempted to examine in depth the conditions that existed in the English prisons; implicitly his exposure of the problems contained recommendations for amelioration. Among the more prominent of Mandeville's suggestions were improved sanitation and ventilation in the cells; separate cells and facilities for men and women; the elimination altogether of the practice of imprisoning debtors; and isolation of the hardened felons from those convicted of lesser crimes. He also proposed the government shorten the length of the time in jail for prisoners awaiting trial; increase the number of judges to accommodate the increasing court dockets; and assign chaplains to all jails and prisons. In addition, Mandeville called for an end to the existing private system of prisons replacing it with publicly-financed institutions; the reduction of the number of death penalties for lesser crimes; an end to public executions; and the abolition of the policy that allowed the sale of alcohol in the prisons. Without exception, Mandeville's suggestions were implemented by John Howard fifty years later in a lasting tribute to the 18th century humanitarian spirit.

Notes

1. John Howard, *The State of the Prisons* (London: J. M. Dent and Sons, Limited, 1929), p. 16.
2. E. N. Williams, *Life in Georgian England* (London: B. T. Batsford, Ltd., 1962), p. 84.
3. Daniel Defoe, *The Shortest Way With the Dissenters* (Stratford-upon-Avon: Shakespeare Head Press, 1928), p. 150.
4. *Ibid.*, pp. 257-258.
5. *Ibid.*, p. 26.
6. Howard, *State of the Prisons*, pp. 2-3.
7. The term "Bridewell" was used to describe a house of correction for the confinement of criminals, paupers, and debtors, so-called from a prison in London at St. Bride's Well.
8. Howard, *State of the Prisons*, pp. 8, 10.
9. H. D. Traill, *Social England* (6 vols; London: Cassell and Company, Ltd., 1897), V, 483.
10. *The Best of Defoe's Review*, ed. William L. Payne (Freeport, New York: Libraries Press, 1951), p. 121.
11. Howard, *State of the Prisons*, p. 8.
12. *Best of Defoe's Review*, pp. 119-122, 208.
13. *Ibid.*, p. 141.
14. *The Works of Henry Fielding, Esq.*, ed. James P. Browne (11 vols; London: Bickers and Son, 1903), X, 345-355, 360, 423-424.
15. Henry Fielding, *The History of Tom Jones, a Foundling* (New York: Heritage Press, 1952), pp. 126, 131.
16. *Works of Fielding*, X, 360.
17. *Works of Fielding*, X, 360.
18. *Best of Defoe's Review*, p. 206.
19. John Trenchard, *Cato's Letters* (4 vols; New York: Russell and Russell, 1969), IV, 236, 241-242.
20. *The Prose Works of Jonathan Swift*, ed. Temple Scoot, Vol. IX, *Contributions to "The Tatler," "The Examiner," "The Spectator," and "The Intelligencer."* (London: C. Bell & Sons, Ltd., 1922), 320.
21. A. P. Herbert, *Mr. Gay's London* (London: Ernest Benn, Limited, 1948), pp. 10, 21.
22. *Prose Works of Swift*, IX, 320.
23. Bernard Mandeville, *An Enquiry into the Causes of the Frequent Executions at Tyburn (1725)* (Los Angeles: University of California, 1964), pp. 1-2, 6-7.

24. *Best of Defoe's Review*, p. 207.
25. Mandeville, *Enquiry*, p. 7.
26. *Ibid.*, p. 17; and H. D. Traill, *Social England* (6 vols; London: Cassell and Company, Ltd., 1897), V, 427.
27. Mandeville, *Enquiry*, p. 17.
28. *Ibid.*, pp. 18-19.
29. Howard, *State of the Prisons*, p. 27.
30. Mandeville, *Enquiry*, p. 19.
31. *Ibid.*, pp. 20-21.
32. *Ibid.*, p. 24.
33. *Ibid.*, pp. 25-27.
34. Andrew Knapp and William Baldwin, *The Newgate Calendar* (2 vols; London: J. Robins and Co., 1824), I, 206-208.
35. Jay Barrett Botsford, *English Society in the Eighteenth Century* (New York: Macmillan Company, 1924), p. 311.
36. Defoe, *Shortest Way*, p. 1.
37. *Memoirs of Howard*, ed. James Baldwin Smith (Boston: Lincoln and Edmunds, 1831), p. 86.
38. Howard, *State of the Prisons*, p. 7.
39. *Memoirs of Howard*, p. 90.
40. Howard, *State of the Prisons*, p. 12; and Traill, *Social England*, p. 483.
41. Howard, *State of the Prisons*, p. 1; and M. Dorothy George, *London Life in the Eighteenth Century* (Harper and Row, Publishers, 1965), pp. 228-229.
42. Howard, *State of the Prisons*, pp. 1, 11.
43. *Ibid.*, p. 10.
44. Mandeville, *Enquiry*, p. 47; and Botsford, *English Society*, p. 142.

5

John Dickinson's Identity Crisis

by
Macel D. Ezell
University of Michigan

With the creation of the British Empire, Englishmen moved out into the far corners of the world, taking with them both the noble and questionable values, attitudes, and styles that had come to characterize citizens of an unusual nation. As individuals they reacted differently to the colonial situations. Some sought to maintain their English ways, determined not to accept change no matter how inappropriate their customs might have seemed in alien environments. Such persons reflected what Charles J. Stille in the late nineteenth century described as "that indefinable but strong feeling of race which gloried in belonging to the foremost nation of modern times."[1] Others, especially the alienated ones and the ones who had been pushed out, welcomed change and deliberately attempted to modify English culture. Still others were caught in the middle, especially prosperous second, third, and later generation colonists who inherited English values without having lived in the mother country. John Dickinson (1732-1808) fits into this third category. Because of his indecision about where his ultimate values lay, he became a controversial figure, who still awaits an adequate biographical study. One of the tasks his biographer will face concerns Dickinson's attempt to square his being an Englishman and an American. In contrast to Jonathan Boucher, whose loyalty never wavered, or Benjamin Franklin, whose pragmatic commitment to the colonial cause apparently gave rise to no great matter of conscience, Dickinson found himself in a dilemma.

In contrast to Dickinson, Benjamin Franklin found an identity as a colonist, as a newcomer to the ranks of the elites, and eventually as an American rather than Englishman. Driven by the appeal of upward mobility, he amassed a fortune in business endeavors rather than by inheriting and expanding a landed estate. He, too, entered politics, but in pragmatic terms rather than out of a sense of noblesse oblige. Instead of developing a finely spun, carefully verbalized political philosophy that tried to combine traditional wisdom and new realities, he could make "accommodations to reality."[2] Rather than agonizing over serious constitutional issues or personal qualms that were raised by the crises between the colonies and the mother country, Franklin "played it safe" until the proper moment arrived. Then he committed himself and became a hero.

Unlike Dickinson and Franklin, Jonathan Boucher (1738-1805) was born in England. Coming to the colonies as a young man, he rose rapidly as a representative of two of the most respected segments of English life: the schools and the church. After beginning his career as a teacher in Virginia, he was ordained an Anglican minister. Soon he became rector of a thriving parish in Annapolis, Maryland, as well as chaplain of the Maryland Assembly. A firm believer in the "sanctity of Established authority," he impressed Moses Coit Tyler as "an old fashioned believer in church and king—in the divine origin and divine authority of government, consequently, in obedience to government as a religious as well as a civil duty."[3] For one so committed to English institutions, there was no problem of choosing sides. From the first he made known his commitment, a loyalty that eventually forced him to return to England rather than risk personal harm because of his political views.

By inheritance Dickinson found himself in a position to enjoy the best of two worlds. Born into an affluent, landed family, he knew a life of ease. Pampered from infancy, he never knew the agonies of poverty, or excessive physical labor, nor had he need to worry about the lack of upward mobility. His inherited Quaker religion put him in good stead in the colonies and did not raise the kinds of bothersome questions for him that Anglican theology did for Boucher. His relative affluence made it possible for him to become one of the best educated men in the colonies. As a student at the Inns of Court in London, he was able to study on a much broader basis than most of his contemporary colonials, whose legal training consisted of "reading" with a lawyer as apprentices.

As a young adult, Dickinson in several ways reflected traits of a cultured English gentleman. In the process of studying in London he became such an able writer that, at least for a time after publication of *Letters from a Pennsylvania Farmer*, he became the voice of colonial Americans. Tyler described him as "the most brilliant event in the literary history of the Revolution."[4] Yet his writing reflected more than an ability to express well the feelings of his fellow Americans: it bore the markings of one well read in the classics, English history, and common law. J. H. Powell has noted that Dickinson "studied the past to derive instruction for the conduct of public affairs."[5] For example, he made this general observation at the end of one of his letters in the *Federalist Papers*: "History sacred and profane tells us, that, *corruption of manners sinks nations into slavery*."[6] Given his training and knowledge of the English heritage, it is not surprising that he wrote a larger number of important political statements on the American cause than did any other colonist.

His writing included far more than his well-known political statements. In typical English fashion of his day, he was an avid pamphleteer. In 1888 Paul Leicester Ford wrote that:

> The English speaking people have been a race of pamphleteers, whenever a question — religious, political, military or personal — has interested the general public, it has occasioned a war of pamphlets, which, however partisan and transitory, were in a manner photographs of the public opinion, and as such have been used and valued by students and publicists.[7]

In addition to pamphlets he also wrote poetry. The Dickinson family papers include several of his poems. And he wrote the lyrics of one of the popular revolutionary songs, "Song for American Freedom." As a speaker, he was also effective. Powell has described him as a "brilliant and popular conversationalist."[8]

Dickinson's social and political status matched that of his affluence and education. As a young man in London he met and occasionally dined with the Penn family and through them met other prominent persons.[9] At home he moved among and was genuinely esteemed by the elite of colonial society, especially that of Philadelphia: "He belonged to the Philadelphia circles which included such old provincial families as the Pembertons, the Logans, and the Norrises."[10] Stanley K. Johannesen has described him as a "social lion."[11] Yet he was not a threatening man; rather he appeared to be somewhat shy and timid.[12] Before he married he was considered to be a preeminently eligible bachelor. Except for the usual partisan comments from political opponents, his entrance into colonial politics was marked by approval, even deference. Eventually he developed one of the largest law practices in Philadelphia.[13] Except for the Declaration of Independence, he had a major voice in the debates concerning, as well as a part in the writing of, the major documents of the era of the Revolution. In short, Dickinson had found a satisfying niche in both English and colonial worlds. The idea of giving up his place in either was far more painful for him than it was for Franklin or Boucher.

The development of tensions between the mother country and the colonies threatened Dickinson's standing in both worlds. At least some of his concerns were economic. Although no one has made detailed studies of his financial affairs nor of his economic theories, it is clear that practical monetary interests had some bearing on his reactions. He undoubtedly realized that changing British colonial policies endangered colonists' economic well-being. He also saw that his interests were intimately tied to both London and Pennsylvania. He did not foresee positive results from a break with the mother country, though. In short, his economic interests would be best served by a continuation of the colonial policies in force before the French and Indian war. He concluded his pamphlet, *The Late Regulations . . . Considered:*

> SHE TEACHES US TO MAKE A DISTINCTION BETWEEN HER INTERESTS AND OUR OWN. Teaches! She requires — commands — insists upon it — threatens — compels — and even distresses us into it.[14]

But more than finances was involved. Over far less controversial issues than independence, Dickinson had found himself embroiled in politics. As a supporter of proprietary rather than royal status for Pennsylvania he had found himself opposing such stalwarts as Joseph Galloway and Benjamin Franklin. Even though he had at times been defeated for political office, he had in the long run been able to survive temporary setbacks relatively unscathed. But when talk of independence arose, he undoubtedly foresaw that he would not be able to survive such a development without permanent scars.

Still more than immediate political status was involved. Records do not indicate that Dickinson ever tried to define just what being an American meant, but his writing frequently refers to the benefits of English citizenship. Although "identity" was not the major issue for colonial Americans that it would become for later generations, Dickinson thought of himself first as an Englishman and then as an American colonist. For one who frequently found solace in turning to the past for answers to bothersome questions the thought of what breaking with inherited traditions, precedents, and institutions would mean in terms of ultimate as well as immediate identity must have been alarming. Yet he also saw the potential advantages of self-rule and the existing drawbacks of a colonial status. Thus he consistently sought to persuade his countrymen so to bear their part in the disputes "as to save their rights as men, without losing their happiness as British subjects."[15]

Given the desirability on Dickinson's part of maintaining both his English and American standings, he was extremely uncomfortable at the notion of having to choose one or the other. Therefore, from the first he wrote and spoke out frequently on the major issues that arose. Since he was highly verbal and influential, it would have been puzzling had he not become a major spokesman after he saw the threats to his way of life. His writings reflect that he exploited both English tradition and American experience to support his moderate opinions. As one versed in and committed to English ways, he reinforced his views by referring to precedents, to law, to the constitution rather than to abstract principles such as those expressed in the Declaration of Independence. To demonstrate his "Americanism" he exploited pastoral agrarian values. Hence he pictured himself not as an English landowner but as a Pennsylvania farmer—humble, reasonable, wise. Consistently he emphasized the importance of attitude, of tone. For example, he "declared that no petition from the colonies had ever been rejected unless it offended the dignity of King or Parliment."[16] He also distrusted emotions that "blind the understanding . . . and weaken the judgment."[17]

Before the final break came, Dickinson's writings dwelt upon two general themes. The first was that colonial grievances were real. From English history he cited numerous cases in which citizens had had cause for complaint. Those in power, he implied, had erred. Unequivocably he criticized the direction of British colonial policies following the French and Indian War. Seldom referring to profit and loss as the major issues, he spoke of rights — of citizens, of Parliament, of the crown. Citing tradition, he constantly encouraged politicians in London to abide by basic, specific precedents.

Even though he recognized threats to colonial rights, he advocated reform rather than revolution as the answer. In essence, he believed that in London, ministers, rather than the king or members of Parliament, were responsible for colonial woes. Hence Parliament and the monarch, he believed, should be told of ministerial errors; he did not doubt that once they saw the problems they would act appropriately. Meanwhile, to bring their grievances to the attention of the authorities in London, he encouraged colonists to form alliances for the purpose of applying economic pressure. Eventually, he argued, the best interests of both parties would be served by conciliation and reform rather than recrimination and rebellion. Tyler has noted that "all his interests and all his tastes [were] on the side of order, conservatism, and peace, if only with these could be had political safety and honor."[18]

Throughout his writings before the Revolution, Dickinson was careful to make clear that he was loyal. One of his strongest affirmations appeared in an address in 1766:

> As to *Great-Britain*, I glory in my relation to her. Every drop of blood in my heart is *British*; and that heart is animated with as warm wishes for her prosperity, as her truest sons can form. As long as this globe continues moving, may she reign over its navigable part.[19]

When the moment for choosing sides came, Dickinson equivocated. A delegate to the Second Continental Congress, he could not bring himself to sign the Declaration of Independence. In response Ezra Stiles suggested:

> He now goes into Oblivion or a dishonorable Reminiscence with Posterity — while the Names of the rest of the Delegates subscribed to the Declaration of Independence are consigned to an honorable Immortality in the History of the United States.[20]

And so far, Stiles' observation has stood unrepudiated. Soon after signing of the Declaration of Independence, a convention removed Dickinson as delegate of Jersey to the Continental Congress. And in Pennsylvania, when a convention appointed officers above Dickinson in the state militia, he resigned his commission. For several months he remained out of public life. But his isolation did not last long. In 1779 he returned to Congress and the Council and House of the Assembly of Delaware elected him president of the state in 1781; in 1782 the Council of Pennsylvania elected him president of that state.[21] He was also a major speaker in the debates which preceded the adoption of the Constitution. During the debates he "boldly asserted . . . that the British constitution had no superior in the world's history."[22] Yet he died "an avowed Jeffersonian."[23]

But all his efforts after 1776 were not effective in restoring him to the place he held in public life before the war. Stiles was correct in foreseeing that Dickinson would not become one of the major heroes of the era. He suffered neither banishment nor financial loss. But the symbolic status he lost in refusing to sign the Declaration of Independence he did not regain. At least partly because of his loss of status, he has received relatively little attention from historians. He has remained, as Johannesen has noted, "the most neglected of the major American Revolutionary figures."[24] When the moment of choosing came, he could not readily give up either part of his loyalty — English or American. For his hesitation he paid the price of temporary disfavor and at least two centuries of relative obscurity.

Notes

1. Charles J. Stille, *The Life and Times of John Dickinson* (Philadelphia: J. B. Lippincott Co., 1891), p. 122.
2. David L. Jacobson, *John Dickinson and the Revolution in Pennsylvania* (Berkeley: University of California Press, 1965), p. 27.
3. Moses Coit Tyler, *The Literary History of the American Revolution*, 2 vols (New York: Frederick Ungar Pub. Co., 1897), I, 323.
4. Ibid., p. 234.
5. J. H. Powell, "John Dickinson and the Constitution," *The Pennsylvania Magazine of History and Biography* 60 (January 1936), 12.
6. John Dickinson, "Letters of Fabius on the Constitution," Number 3, in *Pamphlets of the Constitution of the United States*, ed. Paul Leicester Ford (Brooklyn: n.p., 1888) [Da Capo Press Reprint Edition], p. 180.
7. Ford, *Pamphlets of the Constitution*, p. v.
8. Powell, p. 2.
9. "A Pennsylvania Farmer at the Court of King George: John Dickinson's London Letters, 1754-1756," ed. H. Trevor Colbourn, *The Pennsylvania Magazine of History and Biography* 86 (July 1962), 255, 264, 265.
10. Powell, p. 2.
11. Stanley K. Johannesen, "John Dickinson and the American Revolution," *Historical Reflections* 2 (Summer 1975), 29.
12. Powell, pp. 1-2.
13. Ibid.
14. John Dickinson, *The Late Regulations . . . Reconsidered,* in *The Political Writings of John Dickinson 1764-1774*, ed. Paul Leicester Ford [Reprint Edition] (New York: Da Capo Press, 1970), p. 240.
15. Tyler, I, 234.
16. John C. Miller, *Origins of the American Revolution* (Boston: Little, Brown and Co., 1943), p. 421.
17. John Dickinson, "Speech of May 24, 1764 in the House Assembly of Pennsylvania," in *The Political Writings of John Dickinson 1764-1774*, p. 21.
18. Tyler, I, 235.
19. John Dickinson, "An Address to the Committee of Correspondence in Barbados by a North American," in *The Political Writings of John Dickinson 1764-1774*, p. 267.
20. Cited in Jacobson, p. 117.
21. Powell, pp. 4-5.

22. Ibid., p. 7.
23. Colbourn, Introduction, "A Pennsylvania Farmer at the Court of King George," p. 241.
24. Johannesen, p. 29.

6

Shaftesbury: Crusader for India

by
Margaret Newman Wagers
Southern Methodist University

Much has been written praising the leadership of Anthony Ashley Cooper, Seventh Earl of Shaftesbury (1801-1885), in pioneering great social reforms and humane legislation in nineteenth century England. Yet, little attention has been given to his concern for India and the role he played in the destiny of that faraway subcontinent, upon which he never set foot. When only twenty-six years of age, Lord Ashley, as he was then called, was appointed in 1827 by the new Tory Prime-Minister, the Duke of Wellington, to be a Commissioner on the India Board of Control with the rank of a Junior Minister. An honors graduate of Christ Church, Oxford, he was already noted for his compassion and hard work on the Metropolitan Lunacy Commission, and for his exposure of the Arigna Mining Company Swindle involving several highly placed Tories. Above all, he was known for his unequivocal commitment to Christian principles as the basis for effective and humane public policy.[1] This background was not the kind most likely to commend him to the tough-minded leaders of the Tory Party, but his friend and patron, the Duke of Wellington, was warmly disposed towards this gifted young Dorset neighbor, and insisted on "bringing him forward."[2]

Deeply moved by the confidence placed in him by the Duke, whom he regarded with unquenchable hero-worship, Ashley prayed for guidance in his difficult post and "for the will to discharge my duty and the strength to perform it." Passages from his Diary on his twenty-seventh birthday reveal that he was well aware of the opportunites that lay ahead for him for good or evil: "I . . . behold what mighty interests are entrusted to my care: India, with her hundred millions, is the compass of my mind's survey, and it is almost possible that some happiness or misery may depend upon my principle and vigilance."[3]

In considering his new career, he formulated what should be the basis of his future policy towards India: "The first principle, God's honour; the second, man's happiness; the means, prayer and unremitting diligence." Now, "unremitting diligence" became the order of the day, as for five months he studied India through every available government document, book, or missionary report. His conclusion, after careful reflection as to what his own responsibility and that of Britain should be to their vast Indian colony, was brought to focus in a rhetorical question he addressed to himself: "India: What can I do for your countless myriads? There are two things — good government and Christianity."[4]

He wondered how he could achieve these twin aims since he had, as yet, little influence or eloquence as a speaker, and was only a junior member of a board of cynical middle-aged aristocrats whose reactionary President, Lord Ellenborough, seemed utterly indifferent to any hope of improving the administration of India.[5] It became immediately apparent that Ellenborough, the imperialist, and Ashley, the idealist, had no common ground of understanding. Ashley turned instead to some of the Directors of the East India Company who showed an especial interest in reforming the Indian Government and advancing Christian missions. These men had been deeply affected in the previous two decades, by the Evangelical tradition of William Wilberforce, Charles Grant, and Lord Teignmouth, a former Governor-General of Bengal. The courage and Christian spirit of these merchant Directors heartened Ashley and would be responsible, in part, for his eventual conversion to the Evangelical Movement. He often dined with them informally at the Albion Tavern and welcomed every opportunity to gain their friendship and support.[6] They responded by frankly revealing the deplorable conditions existing in India under an unstructured and divisive British regime.

From the eighteenth century onwards, the control of Indian affairs had been divided between the independent East India Company with its Directors and the Commissioners on the India Board of Control, who supervised the East India Company and served as intermediaries between the Government at home and in India. There was also a Governor-General nominated by the Crown and the Ministry to preside over Bengal, and to a lesser extent, over the Presidency of Madras, Bombay and the other English portions of India. Fortunately for Ashley's benign intentions, the new Governor-General of Bengal, Sir William Cavendish Bentinck, had been appointed under the recent Canning Coalition Government and was an experienced administrator of liberal views, who was determined to govern India justly for the benefit of its people, rather than carry out a policy of commercial and imperial exploitation.

Lord Ellenborough, however, coveted the post of Governor-General and had the backing of Wellington and the majority of the Board of Control in his efforts to discredit and recall Bentinck as a "Canningite interloper" on any pretext he could devise. The unsuspecting Bentinck, after almost half a year's voyage, arrived at last in Bengal in July, 1828, to find Wellington already installed in office at home, and a most precarious political and economic situation in India. Although Britain's territories were now at peace, the recent war with Burma under Lord Amherst had resulted in an annual deficit to the Government of a million pounds sterling.[7]

Bentinck was ordered by the Court of Directors to economize drastically and balance the budget by reducing all allowances, which, under the name of "butta" had for many years been given to European officers in addition to their pay. In this fashion, Ellenborough had thought to make Bentinck so unpopular with the English officers that he could not function. Bentinck, however, survived the officers' complaints and showed a genius for finance, eventually achieving a two million pound surplus by hiring natives at lower salaries to posts hitherto reserved exclusively for more highly paid Englishmen in the Government.[8] His effacing of "humiliating distinctions" between Englishmen and Indians made him respected and effective among the Indian people. He built up an excellent and loyal native civil service by setting up English type schools for the requisite training, although Lord Ellenborough and the Board, with the exception of Ashley, disapproved of his action.

As famine was a constant threat to India, Ashley was especially concerned in enlarging India's food supplies and suggested to the Board the foundation of "Scientific Corporations for the Institution and Improvement of Horticulture and Husbandry Throughout the Provinces of India." The introduction of new vegetables and fruits suitable to the Indian soil and climate was urged as well. He showed an especial enthusiasm for the cultivation of the potato, whose new varieties offered possible alternatives to rice, which was the main, often, the sole crop of the country.[9] He also took up the question of the government's salt monopoly, which bore most unfairly and oppressively upon the Indian people.

While engaging in such practical matters, Ashley, whose hobby was astronomy, sought successfully to encourage further astronomical research, by persuading the Deputy-chairman of the East India Company to set up an observatory in Bombay.

Meanwhile, Ashley was assigned the thankless task of reviewing English laws and legal procedures as they pertained to India so that they might be brought up to date and reformed. English Courts of Appeal in India had been scandalously slow in dealing with litigation and often the decisions rendered were inconsistent with one another and with precedent. Ashley expended "long and wearing toil" on this enterprise, which seemed so important to him and Bentinck, but which was lightly regarded by Ellenborough, who complained on several occasions "that Ashley came and bored me."[10] Although no lawyer himself, Ashley had sought expert legal opinion and advice, but when he submitted his memorandum to Lord Ellenborough, the latter haughtily rejected its proposals without explanation.[11] Ashley was determined, however, to introduce the matter of judicial reform for India in the House of Commons. There he made such a convincing speech that it caused the testy old economist, Joseph Hume, to remark that he was surprised to hear so much good sense from the noble Lord "or indeed from any member of His Majesty's Government."[12] Encouraged by his successful reception in the Commons, Ashley sent his proposals on judicial reform to Bentinck, who made good use of them. The latter had long since discovered that the intelligent and hard-working Ashley was his only real supporter on the India Board, and that the young man was a redoubtable ally in molding public opinion in the press, among the East India Company Directors, and in the powerful London and World Missionary and Bible Societies. The Governor-General and Ashley carried on a warm and confidential correspondence as frequently as the era's slow-moving ships would allow. Many of the ideas from Ashley's "Jury Minute" found their way into Bentinck's new administrative policy, where he allowed natives to take their place as judges and jurors in the lower civil courts. In time, Bentinck revised the whole judicial system in the direction of Ashley's original suggestions for obtaining faster and surer justice for all, whether English or native.

Another source of gratification to Ashley on the India Board was that he had won an assurance of protection for Christian missionaries, and for the first time, the right to inherit property for converts to Christianity from Hinduism and Islam. "God Almighty be praised!" exulted Ashley in his diary on March 27, 1829, "We have at last established a new order of things for British India . . . Am I too sanguine?" He was, indeed, too sanguine, for Lord Ellenborough had been searching relentlessly for a method of discarding Bentinck, and thought he had found the weapon to accomplish his purpose, when his Governor-General suggested abolishing Suttee. Ashley later in life recalled the struggle he had as an ally of Bentinck's against the inhuman practice of burning Indian widows alive on the funeral pyres of their dead husbands: "I recollect perfectly well, when I was on the India Board in 1828, on the question of Sutteeism . . . coming before us, thinking it a matter of most outrageous cruelty and wrong. On saying so, I was put down at once as if I were a madman; I was wondered at for even daring to mention such a thing."[13] Ellenborough, Wellington, and Ashley's other colleagues on the India Board opposed terminating Suttee on the grounds that British treaty agreements accepted Hindu and Moslem religious practices, and that a great uprising might result among native troops should interference occur.[14] If the Board could get rid of Bentinck on this issue, so much the better, for the Governor-General seemed determined to pursue his own course, irrespective of their fears and wishes.

Under Moslem rule, Bentinck was shocked to discover that the practice of Suttee had been discouraged, but under the British regime, the horrible rite had grown to such an extent that 10,000 widows died in this fashion in Bengal alone during 1828, the year of the new Governor-General's arrival. Indeed, the cruel ceremony had spread and increased in the lower provinces where, in the first year of Bentinck's administration, 800 widows suffered Suttee as contrasted to an annual average of 600 for the preceding ten years.[15] Bentinck wisely began his campaign against Suttee by winning the support of the Nizamet Adaalait (High Hindu Court of India), and by polling the English and native army officers, the police, and a great number of public functionaries, the majority of whom were against the practice. Many of the Directors of the East India Company abhorred Suttee, but Ellenborough and the Board of Control, claiming that Bentinck was rashly precipitating a mutiny, determined to send him a unanimous vote of censure, which would be tantamount to a recall. Much pressure was brought on Ashley by Ellenborough either to censure or to resign as a Commissioner. In this crisis, Charles Arbuthnot, the Duke of Wellington's assistant, wrote a strong letter hinting dismissal if Ashley did not comply, but the latter stood firm in his refusal to sign the "insulting despatch" to Bentinck. "It may end in my dismissal from office," he wrote, "but I shall have acted in good conscience."[16] He wondered, however, if he would have been as brave if he had had a family to support. Actually, Ashley paid a high price for his stand on Suttee, for he lost the thing he valued most, which was the Duke's friendship and esteem. Wellington had been like a father to Ashley, but the "Iron Duke" would never again admit the young man to the intimacy of his inner circle. This was particularly harsh because Lord Shaftesbury, the ultra-conservative Chairman on Committees in the House of Lords had denounced his son the previous February when Ashley dared support the Duke and Robert Peel by speaking in behalf of their controversial Catholic Emancipation Bill. Now having lost both his father's and the Duke's goodwill and patronage, Ashley found his own political future further impaired by Ellenborough's animosity and by Peel's conviction that Ashley was no longer a "reliable party man."

Ashley's troubles were further augmented in August, 1829, when he fell in love with the spirited and charming Minny Cowper, daughter of Earl Cowper, the Whig magnate. Dismissal now from the Board of Control would not only occasion his open disgrace, but cause Ashley to lose his yearly stipend of a thousand pounds, without which he could scarcely hope to convince Earl Cowper to let him marry his daughter. Ashley's father further humiliated him by ordering him home to St. Giles House to give him an insulting tongue-lashing for what he termed the young man's "humanity mongering" on the India Board. Ashley was plunged in despair, and it was with difficulty that Minny Cowper restrained him from giving up his position to seek a new life in America.[17] Fortunately, on December 4, 1829, Bentinck courageously took the responsibility on his own shoulders of abolishing Suttee by an order in Council in Calcutta, making it punishable in the Criminal Courts as homicide.[18] None of the public disorders of mutinies feared by Ellenborough and Wellington resulted, and later Ashley described with satisfaction the public reaction: "My Lord William Bentinck . . . with a stroke of his pen, put the unnatural practice down, and the whole of India was satisfied that it was right . . . if you appeal to the conscience, depend upon it, the millions will go along with you."[19]

Certainly the imagination of middle-class England was enormously stirred when the news that Suttee had been abolished finally arrived from India and was broadcast in the press. Bentinck was lauded on all sides.[20] Ashley, basking in some of the reflected glory, was able to marry Minny Cowper, but lost his position on the India Board in 1830, when the Government was dissolved at the death of George IV. He always retained a keen interest, however, in Indian affairs both in Parliament, and through his leadership in various missionary and Bible societies, which offered backing to enlightened statesmen in India, such as Sir William Bentinck, Sir Henry Lawrence, Sir Henry Havelock, and many other conscientious public servants. Bentinck was appointed in 1833 the first Governor-General for *all* of British India and served with distinction and acclaim until the impaired state of his health caused him to retire to England in 1835.

Though loving the Indian people, neither Ashley nor Bentinck had any patience with the "abominable incrustations of Hinduism" when expressed through ceremonies of torture and death. Soon Bentinck curbed the murderous hand of the Thugs and their cult of Thugee. It must be remembered that in the 1820's, multitudes of human victims were annually sacrificed upon the altars of Hindu pilgrim centers at Guya, Allalahabad, Tripetz, and Juggernaut, all within the territories of the East India Company. The company derived, over a fifteen year period, a net profit of over a million pounds sterling for giving protection to this carnage for organizing pilgrimages and remunerating "pilgrim hunters" at so much a head, for keeping the temples in repair, supporting the priests, and for imposing a large tax at the four shrines for the votaries to gain admittance. It was estimated that 1,200,000 persons traveled to Juggernaut each year. Many perished under the wheels of the idol's mammoth chariot, but most died from the arduous long journey, the heat, the pestilence and famine, so that it was estimated that only ten percent ever returned home to their families. The worship of Juggernaut, which had dwindled under Muslim rule, was made popular again under the British Regime that the town and its pilgrims had doubled in size.[21] By the middle of the century, however, Lord Ashley was able to announce that Britain's sponsorship and toleration of these barbarous but lucrative Hindu rites had ceased.[22]

The years 1842 and 1843 saw Ashley locking horns again with his old adversary, Lord Ellenborough. Ashley was carried to a feverish pitch of indignation by two simultaneous wars which he thought outrageously unjust and shameful. The first was the war with Afghanistan, being conducted by Lord Ellenborough, now appointed the new Governor-General of India. The second was the Opium War with China, also waged and directed from Indian bases by Ellenborough, which ended in the humiliation of China in the Treaty of Nanking.[23] Ashley thought that the latter war, fought to smuggle opium into China against the wishes of the Chinese Government, was one of the "most lawless, unnecessary and unfair struggles in history," and he confided to his Diary on November 15, 1842: "Christians have shed more blood in two years than Heathens have shed Christian blood in two centuries . . . The peace, too, is as wicked as the war! We refuse even now to give the Emperor of China relief in the matter of the opium trade."

Urged on by his Quaker friends, Samuel Gurney and William Fry, Lord Ashley agreed to expose the whole opium conspiracy in the Commons and on April 4, 1843, he presented a petition against the opium traffic from the Committees of the Wesleyan,

Baptist, and London Missionary Societies, moving that the trade be abolished "as destructive of all relations of amity between England and China, injurious to the legitimate manufacturing interests and trade of Britain, . . . and utterly inconsistent with the honour and duties of a Christian Kingdom." In a devastating speech, Ashley argued that the substitution of opium for the rightful manufactures of Britain had weakened legitimate trade with China and given England a bad name throughout the world. Furthermore, it had not only demoralized the Chinese people but addicted the Indian ryots (peasants) as well, who were relentlessly pressured, and often compelled to accept Government grants in advance to supply the needed quantity of poppy, even though its cultivation wore out their land and reduced their food supply. It was then the imperial policy of England to carry the opium to Calcutta and put it up for sale to be shipped in opium clippers, supplied with cannon and arms from British arsenals and manned by desperate smugglers and criminals capable of forcing their way into China. Ashley observed that this nefarious trade was even worse than the slave trade. "Slavery," he said, "tortures and degrades the man but it leaves him susceptible of regeneration. But the opium trade destroys the man, both body and soul; and carries a hideous ruin for millions which can never be repaired."[24] A debate ensued in the House, those opposing Ashley arguing that opium was no worse than alcohol and it would be ridiculous to lose the revenue, since if Britain gave it up, some other country such as Turkey would be sure to supply it. Sir Robert Peel, as Prime Minister, defended the Government's position on the opium traffic and blandly sabotaged Ashley's motion by saying it would jeopardize the Supplementary Peace Treaty he was in the process of negotiating with China. The subject of the opium trade, however, had been brought to the attention of Parliament, and discussed throughout all England, receiving very good coverage in the press and particularly *The Times*.

Nevertheless, through the next decade, England still sanctioned the shameful opium traffic, and the evil grew. In 1856 the Chinese authorities arrested some opium smugglers, many of them recognized Chinese criminals, on a vessel called the "Arrow" flying the British flag, but which was really a Chinese craft. Although China gave way to Britain's ultimatum within the time limit set, Britain imposed a second crushing war upon her, causing Richard Cobden to initiate a vote of censure in the Commons against Palmerston's government on February 26. Ashley, now the Seventh Earl of Shaftesbury since he had succeeded to his father's seat in the Lords in 1851, viewed this as a political ruse on the part of the opposition factions to oust Palmerston while sedulously avoiding the crucial subject of the opium traffic. Therefore, on March 9, Shaftesbury made a speech introducing the question of the illegality of the opium trade into the House of Lords, and urging the Lord Chancellor to submit the matter to the Judges for their opinion.[25] Instead, the Lord Chancellor consulted the Law Officers of the Crown, who declared unanimously that such trade was legal, and no violation of the treaty with China. Shaftesbury, however, crusaded the remainder of his life, though unsuccessfully, as President of the Anti-Opium League to end the evils from this drug.[26]

Shaftesbury, meanwhile, was again turning his attention to Afghanistan, where Ellenborough was wreaking havoc with everything the former held most sacred. Pushed back in Afghanistan, Lord Ellenborough and Lord Napier, the Governor of Sind, provoked the friendly Amirs of Sind into war and defeat in 1843, and then tried to annex Gwalior, as well. In the House of Lords Shaftesbury denounced this treachery against England's friendly allies, and the Directors of The East India Company, exasperated by Ellenborough's "arrogant self-will" and "rash opportunism", recalled him in 1844. Nevertheless, the aftermath of the great Sepoy Mutiny of 1857, which saw so many thousands of British nationals massacred and so many Christian missions wiped out, found Ellenborough back in control as President of the India Board. The Conservative Ministry entrusted him with the drafting of a new plan for the government of India, which the Indian Mutiny had made necessary. Shaftesbury as representative and leader of many important religious and missionary societies tried in vain to have the "claims of Christianity" recognized meaningfully, either in the instrument of Government, or in the Proclamation that went with it to the people of India. Ellenborough blocked this request but his power was waning. Politically jealous of Lord Canning, the new Viceroy of India, Ellenborough tried to weaken the Viceroy's hand by censuring him publicly for proclaiming the confiscation of the property of the rebellious native landed proprietors of Oude, who had not yet made their submission to the English authorities. This caustic censure aroused so much opposition from Shaftesbury and others in the House of Lords that Ellenborough chose to resign.[27]

Five years later, in 1861, when the United States was convulsed by Civil War and it became obvious that the cotton supply would fail, causing great hardship to English mills, Shaftesbury brought forth a vast project he had long contemplated to benefit both India and Britain. India, long accustomed to the cultivation of cotton, had let her production run down, due to drought, famine, and poor transportation. To remove the danger of famine from India in the future and to insure a permanent supply of good cotton for English mills, Shaftesbury, on July 3, 1861, moved an address to the Crown "to give serious attention to extending to India the best possible systems of irrigation and internal navigation." In a remarkably well researched speech, Shaftesbury attributed the famines in India to the fact "that rivers, irrigation, streams, and canals had become obstructed: the tanks and water-courses—the glory of native princes—had become the reproach of their successors." The British had allowed them to deteriorate and, in the process, the riches and fertility of India had been diminished.[28] Quoting facts and figures from Britain's foremost engineers, he showed the advantages gained on projects already undertaken, and estimated how work on future water projects would add from three to sixfold to the productiveness of the land, which, he said, was far better than annexing additional territory. It would enhance the wealth of India, enable her to feed her people, ensure cheap water transportation, augment British revenue from taxes, give a continuous cotton supply and a market for British manufactures, as well as "teaching America that the cotton industry could be profitably run by the unshackled endeavors of freemen." He concluded with an appeal to responsible action: "My Lords, by the conquest . . . of the country, we have torn from the natives any means of improving their own financial condition, of regulating their own internal affairs, of advancing, unaided, their own interests. Our duty then is clear."[29]

Shaftesbury was not supported in the Lords probably as a result of the high cost of his proposed enterprise, the popularity of the

Malthusian doctrine, and the great influence of the Railroad lobby, which was promoting Indian Railway bonds and stocks, and which did not wish to meet competition from cheap water transportation.[30] Shaftesbury was, however, more successful in bringing an important piece of humanitarian factory legislation to fruition in 1879, even though he was then seventy-eight years old and speaking before a "hostile ministry and an unsympathetic House." The aged crusader, on April 4, 1879, held the floor of the House of Lords by his eloquence for over an hour, moving "that her Majesty would be graciously pleased to instruct the Viceroy of India to take into immediate consideration the necessity of passing a law regulating the labour of women and children in the mills and factories throughout her dominions in India." Through successive administrations, Shaftesbury had been pointing out the great need for such legislation. Horrible as the conditions of factory labour had once been in England, those prevailing in India were indescribably worse, since there was no religious sentiment setting aside a weekly day of rest and little regard for the individual.[31]

The evidence introduced by Shaftesbury showed conclusively that women and children from the earliest ages stood working in a poisonous atmosphere of 90-95 degrees Fahrenheit, from eleven to sixteen hours a day, with only fifteen to thirty minutes of rest allowed at noon. There were no safety precautions, and cleanliness and provisions for sanitation were almost non-existent. In one factory visited in Bombay by an Englishman, the guide asserted that the machinery had been run steadily for years with never a rest-stop for the workers, as the native proprietors would think it a loss of time. "Sunday and week-days, rain or sunshine, the continued grind went on without intermission from one year's end to the other. Flesh and blood, coal or steam—it is all one to the native millowner! 'Get as much out of them as you can' is their way."[31] Some Indian mothers were even forced to bring their babies to the mills and "lay them under the looms as they plied their work, thus putting the infants in great jeopardy of health." Pitying these exploited women, Shaftesbury exclaimed, "Of all the classes who toil for livelihood, there is none so helpless and friendless and subdued as these wretched women. They are doubly slaves—slaves to the millowners and to their husbands, who, disregarding their sufferings, revel at ease in their hard-won earnings."[32] To Shaftesbury's surprise and gratification, the speech met with great success, resulting in the Government's giving its support to the first factory legislation ever passed for Indian workers.[33]

It is difficult to evaluate the total impact of Shaftesbury's contribution to India. In common with Sir William Bentinck and Sir Henry Lawrence, he had a great sense of duty and Christian stewardship. These men, educated in the classical tradition of imperial Greece and Rome, were convinced that they carried with them the torch of civilization and endured no qualms when imposing their culture on alien races. Through the benefits of Christianity and the rule of law, they believed they were giving the best they had to offer to subject peoples, as well as educating them and preparing them for constitutional self-government. Shaftesbury, particularly, looked forward to a time when India, converted to Christian ideals and British forms of government, would enjoy complete autonomy within the British Commonwealth. Therefore, he risked Queen Victoria's wrath by opposing, in 1876, Disraeli's bid to bestow upon her the title "Empress of India," on the grounds that it offended constitutional sentiment and smacked of despotism and militarism. He took this occasion to voice his hope for the future of India, declaring that "a time may come when, after a long course of happy rule, we may surrender India to natives grown into a capability for self-government."[34] To attain this end, he maintained that the Indians must first be educated in British principles and imbued with British feelings and sentiments. For this purpose, he advocated extension of Christian missions and of the system of British-style schools and colleges at all levels in India. He also urged his countrymen to welcome Indian students to British universities and technical colleges warmly and enthusiastically.[35] He deplored the condescension and what he termed "the rigid characteristics of English behaviour," which marred the attitude of the majority of English public servants toward Indians.

Shaftesbury believed that India and other British dependencies should be rigorously trained for future independence, and this was his goal throughout his life: "I should like to make each colony, so far as possible, a transcript of the Mother Country," he asserted; "I would protect and train it into its riper years, and then give it, like a full-grown son, free action and absolute independence."[36] His optimism was always tempered, however, with a due regard for the fallibility and corruptness of human nature, whether English or Indian, and sometimes in his diary, he struck a note of caution: "England was to have been the fountain, and our globe the soil to have been watered by her: may she do it yet, though I fear unless God administer the healing branch, the stream will be very corrupt."[37]

Notes

1. Diary of the Seventh Earl of Shaftesbury, March 4, April 1, 4, 9, 11, 1827, Broadlands Archives MS., SHA/PD/1, at the Royal Commission on Historical Manuscripts, Quality House, London. Lord Mountbatten of Burma, the present Earl of Shaftesbury, and the trustees of the Broadlands Archives gave permission to use Shaftesbury's handwritten diaries and private papers. (Hereafter, the diary manuscripts will be referred to as Shaftesbury's Diary.) Also see Hansard, 2nd series, XVII, 333, on Arigna Mining Company Report.
2. *The Correspondence of Charles Arbuthnot*, ed. A. Aspinall (London: Royal Historical Society, 1941), p. 119.
3. Shaftesbury's Diary, April 28, 1828.
4. Ibid., August 3, 1828.
5. Edward Law, Earl of Ellenborough (1790-1871). See *Dictionary of National Biography*, ed. Sydney Lee (London: Smith, Elder and Co., 1892), XXXII, 222-4.
6. William Wilberforce, Charles Grant, and Lord Teignmouth (John Shore) were members of the Evangelical Movement and belonged to the Clapham Group, sometimes derisively called "The Saints." This group took the lead in abolishing slavery, in pioneering causes of social justice in Parliament, and in establishing overseas Christian missions. Lord Ashley joined the Evangelical Movement about 1834, and soon became its leader, since Wilberforce had died the previous year. See G.F.A. Best, *Shaftesbury* (London: B. T. Batsford, 1964), p. 54 and E. M. House, *The Saints in Politics* (London: George Allen and Unwin, 1953), pp. 23-5.
7. Demetrius C. Boulgar, *Rulers of India: Bentinck* (Oxford: Clarendon Press, 1892), pp. 96-7. (Hereafter referred to as *Bentinck*.)
8. Ibid., p. 100.
9. Edwin Hodder, *The Life and Work of the Seventh Earl of Shaftesbury, K. G.* (London: Cassell and Co., 1886), I, 83. (Hereafter referred to as *Shaftesbury*.)
10. Georgina Battiscombe, *Shaftesbury: A Biography of the Seventh Earl, 1801-1885* (London: Constable, 1974), p. 43.
11. Shaftesbury's Diary, December 20, 1828.
12. Barbara Blackburn, *Noble Lord* (London: Home and Van Thal, 1949), p. 31.
13. Hodder, *Shaftesbury*, I, 82.

14. Wellington and Ellenborough believed Bentinck had been responsible for a mutiny ending in the massacre of British officers at Vellore in 1806. See Boulgar, *Bentinck*, pp. 110-1.
15. Ibid., p. 83. Also see House's *The Saints in Politics*, p. 60, citing Wilberforce's evidence in 1813 in his India Bill Speech that the number of widows burned in the Calcutta area alone had doubled in the one year span between 1802-1803 under British rule.
16. Shaftesbury's Diary, July 26, 1829.
17. Ibid., October 8, 1829. Also see Aspinall's *Correspondence of Charles Arbuthnot*, p. 119, and Hampshire County Archives, Broadlands Papers 27/M/60, Box L.
18. In 1830 the Act was extended to Madras and Bombay, and in June 1832 it was ratified by the Privy Council. See *The Government Gazette*, Calcutta, Dec. 7, 1829 and *The Greville Diary*, ed. Philip Williams-Wilson (London: William Henneman, 1927), II, 314-5.
19. Hodder, *Shaftesbury*, I, 82.
20. The general spirit of adulation felt for Bentinck was reflected in a poem, "The Suttee," written by William E. Gladstone while a senior at Christ Church, Oxford. In British Museum, see Gladstone Papers. Add. MSS. 44720, f. 121.
21. The Rev. William Thorpe, "England's Apostasy in India" (A Course of Lectures Delivered in Bristol in 1827), parts of which were appended to *The Earl of Shaftesbury's Great Speech on Indian Cruelties, Delivered at Wimborne, Oct. 30, 1857*. (London: Partridge and Co. and Robert Banks and Co., 1857), pp. 2-5 of Appendix.
22. Edwin Hodder, *Life and Work of the Seventh Earl of Shaftesbury, K. G.*, Popular Edition (London: Cassell and Co., 1887), p. 546.
23. J. Wesley Bready, *Lord Shaftesbury and Social Industrial Progress* (London: Allen and Unwin, 1926), p. 342.
24. *On the Suppression of the Opium Trade: The Speech of the Right Hon. Lord Ashley, M.P., in the House of Commons on Tuesday, April 4, 1843*. (London: Houlston and Stoneman, 1843), p. 37.
25. Bready, *Lord Shaftesbury*, p. 359; Shaftesbury's speeches in House of Lords, March 9, May 14, June 22, Aug. 20, Aug. 24, 1857. Hansard, 3rd series, CXLV. Some writers have criticized Shaftesbury for voting with the Government, to support Lord Palmerston who was the step-father of Lady Shaftesbury, but fail to mention, however, that Shaftesbury made a courageous speech against the opium traffic only a week after Cobden's motion of censure. See, for example, J. L. and Barbara Hammond, *Lord Shaftesbury* (Harmondsworth, Middlesex: Penguin Books, 1923) p. 224.
26. In October, 1881, Shaftesbury, now eighty years old, made one of his strongest indictments against the opium traffic. As late as 1924, En-

gland still derived an income of four million pounds sterling from this death-dealing trade, and Singapore received forty-three percent of all its revenue from opium. See Bready, *Lord Shaftesbury*, p. 363, and "The Opium Failure", *The Nation*, December 27, 1924.

27. Edwin Hodder, *Life and Work of the Seventh Earl of Shaftesbury, K.G.*, Pop. Ed. (London: Cassell and Co., 1887), p. 549.
28. Unlike Shaftesbury, most British officials adhered to Malthusian principles of non-intervention in famines. At Orissa, in 1866, when a quarter of the population died of hunger, the members of the Board of Revenue there refused to import grain and would not even allow the authorities to take grain from a ship that ran ashore and rotted on their coast. See Garth Lean, *Brave Men Choose* (London: Blandford Press, 1961), p. 52.
29. Anthony A. Cooper, Earl of Shaftesbury, *Speeches of the Seventh Earl of Shaftesbury* (London: Chapman and Hall, 1868, reprinted by the Irish University Press, Shannon, Ireland, 1971), pp. 356-7.
30. It is of interest today that the United Nations Development Program is now working out ways to help India in almost exactly the same plan of irrigation works, dams, reservoirs and canals as Shaftesbury envisaged in 1861. It will be the world's greatest water project, costing an estimated 4,000 million dollars, and will take at least twenty-five years to complete. See "World's Largest Water Project," *Christian Science Monitor*, October 6, 1972, p. 1.
31. The Hindu holidays are only about fourteen in a year, with no Sundays for rest. See Hansard, 3rd series, CCXIV, 350.
32. Hansard, 3rd series, CCXIV, 354.
33. Hansard, 3rd series, CCXIV, 378. Also see Bready, *Lord Shaftesbury and Social-Industrial Justice*, p. 339.
34. House of Lords, April 3, 1878 (Shaftesbury makes amendment to the Royal Title Speech), quoted in Hodder, *Shaftesbury*, III, 370.
35. Cooper, *Speeches of the Earl of Shaftesbury*, p. 369.
36. Shaftesbury's Diary, November 25, 1845.
37. Ibid., April 28, 1826.

7

W. H. T. Gairdner: An Englishman in Egypt

by
Lawrence R. Murphy
University of Illinois

Nearly every eye turned to watch the man who wheeled his bicycle onto a Cairo street. Most of those who crowded the narrow passageways wore long, colorful gowns reaching almost to the ground, their heads wrapped in white turbans. A few, the *effendis*, dressed in European-style clothes and covered their heads with Turkish tarbushes. The women, many veiled, nearly hid themselves in black velveteen. Melodic Arabic voices permeated the air, interrupted only rarely by French or English words. Animals added to the cacophony — water buffalos, donkeys, horses, camels. The focus of everyone's stares seemed to be an Englishman, not unusual in a country long ruled by Britain. According to custom, he pushed through the crowd and steered through the city reading a book or newspaper (usually in Arabic) perched on the handlebars. He must be a churchman, for English civil officials never wore the kind of dark robes that flew behind "like a black sail."[1] From 1899 until his death in 1928, this man, William Henry Temple Gairdner, was a familiar scene on the streets of Cairo as he dedicated his life to the Christian evangelization of Egypt.

Born at the Scottish country town of Androssen in 1873, Gairdner was the eldest son of Sir William Tenant Gairdner, a distinguished physician and medical professor at Edinburgh University, who was knighted in 1898. Temple, as the eldest son was called, shared many of his father's scholarly and aesthetic interests, and at the age of nineteen enrolled at Trinity College, Oxford. Classical studies attracted him: Greek statues adorned his room, and he became so immersed in language and literature that he sometimes felt that "half my soul is Greek." His love of music also grew. Other talented students became close friends. "He was at Oxford with [diplomat] Sir John Simon, [jurist and politician] Lord Birkenhead, and [historian] Hilaire Belloc," a friend recalled, "and he was the greatest of them all, and the most richly endowed."[2] Above all, Oxford instilled in Gairdner a continuing interest in learning. "If a man goes down from college without having acquired the habit of study," he noted in a speech delivered to his undergraduate colleagues, "he will never acquire it."[3]

At Oxford Gairdner became increasingly religious. During the Christmas holidays in 1892, his younger brother Hugh fell ill, and Temple watched him die. The experience produced a dramatic religious awakening. "When I knelt by Hugh's bed," Temple explained, "I felt the necessity of putting Christ first and the rest nowhere . . . henceforth there could be but one duty for me, to follow where I heard Him calling." When he returned to school, Temple joined the Christian Student Union, a campus organization modeled after the American Student Volunteer Movement for Foreign Missions. Together with a close friend, Douglas M. Thornton, Gairdner became active in the Volunteer Missionary Union. Following graduation, both went to work on the staff of the organization.[4]

Both Thornton and Gairdner eventually wanted to work overseas among non-Christians. China? India? The Near East? Gradually, their interest focused on the Nile Valley. In 1884 General Charles G. "Chinese" Gordon had led a British expedition up the Nile to the Sudan. The next January, after a long seige by Moslem rebels at Khartoum, Gordon's troops had been defeated, and he died. As English newspapers asked Christians to pray for Gordon, Gairdner vowed someday to work in the Sudan to honor his memory. Thornton, less romantic, saw Cairo as the educational center of the Moslem world, an ideal place in which to work among students. Both men volunteered for service with the Church Missionary Society's Egypt mission. Thornton left for Cairo soon after being ordained, arriving in November 1898. Gairdner followed later the next year.[5]

Despite the growing influence of Europe, Cairo was still the largest and most important city in the Moslem world. Nearby were the major monuments of ancient Egypt. With its historic mosques, crumbling military fortifications, and narrow winding streets, the city retained a medieval Islamic character. More than ninety percent of the people were Moslems who devoutly read the Holy Koran, prayed toward Mecca at the prescribed hours, and looked to their religious leaders for social, political, and spiritual direction. A small percentage were Christian, but their Coptic Orthodox beliefs bore little resemblance to the European Christianity of Gairdner and Thornton. Despite its seeming backwardness, Cairo was an intellectual center. For centuries Moslems from throughout the world had studied at its famed Al-Azhar University, where the most learned Islamic divines gave instruction. The city's printing presses produced books, magazines, and newspapers for much of the Arabic-speaking world.

Beginning during the reign of Mohammed Ali early in the nineteenth century, Egypt had modernized through the adoption of European concepts concerning agriculture, technology, education, and government. True, most Egyptians, especially rural peasants, were little affected by such changes, but an entire class, the powerful *effendis*, had adopted European styles and modes of life. They often spoke French, and many had studied in or at least visited Europe. A few rejected Islam, and more demanded progressive interpretations of its precepts.

England had a special role in Egypt. Using a native protest led by Ahmed Orabi Pasha as a pretext, in 1882 British troops occupied the valley of the Nile and seized effective control of the country. The English language and methods dominated official life. The Church Missionary Society had played a limited although not insignificant part in the modernization of Egypt. The CMS sent five German workers to Cairo in 1825, but they were limited to evangelistic efforts among Copts. Only one man remained after 1852, and a decade later the mission officially closed. In 1882, as English troops occupied Egypt, the CMS returned, hoping that a more cooperative British government would enable them to work freely among Moslems.

The arrival of Thornton and Gairdner in Cairo initiated an important expansion of the Egyptian mission. The ultimate objective of all missionaries was conversion, not, as an 1897 letter of instruction made clear, "merely from one religious system to another, but from darkness to light, from sin to righteousness, from lust to purity, from the slavery of Satan to the liberty of Christ."[6] This was most difficult among highly sophisticated people who held their religious beliefs deeply and strongly. Soon after arriving in Cairo, Thornton wrote Gairdner that the Moslem world was "the line of greatest resistance . . . the last that is likely to yield."[7]

Early CMS work through hospitals or schools had been relatively unsuccessful, and the few converts had been unsophisticated individuals from the lower levels of society. Thornton and Gairdner hoped to work among students and other educated, influential Moslems. Presumably two well-educated, intelligent Britishers should be as successful among Islamic students as the Student Volunteer Movement had been among young scholars in England and America. Learned discussions, debates, lectures, tracts, pamphlets, and magazines would all help confront Egyptians with what were to Gairdner and Thornton the obvious advantages of Christianity.[8]

While these beliefs smacked of a certain arrogance that permeated nearly all missionary activity, young missionaries were ironically expected to humble themselves before their elders and superiors. The CMS operated with a quasi-military organization. Ultimate authority rested with a committee of churchmen and lay volunteers in London. Each mission had its own executive committee composed of senior missionaries. Only in rare cases could individual missionaries communicate directly with London. New workers were expected to respect the opinions of their predecessors and elders. "Should it happen that such work and plans appear to be in any measure misguided," Gairdner's standard letter of instruction recommended, "you [should] nevertheless go with thorough heartiness into them," hoping eventually to discover "the real facts of the case."[9]

Soon after leaving England, Gairdner discovered just how much obedience was expected. As mission secretary F. F. Adney pointed out, Gairdner was "not at all a man to manage for himself." His friends concluded that finding a wife and setting up his own household was the best solution for Gairdner's domestic situation. Gairdner had in mind a girl whom he had known since childhood, Margaret Mitchell. When she accepted his marriage proposal in mid-1902, he was overjoyed. "Something heavenly, something spiritual," he hoped would come from their marriage.[10]

Matrimony was no simple matter for missionaries, however. According to CMS regulations, the wedding could not be approved until both man and woman had spent a year in service. Miss Mitchell must, therefore, learn Arabic and do proselytizing work for twelve months. Gairdner appealed the ruling, but neither the older men in Cairo nor the committee in London was sympathetic. They ordered Miss Mitchell to Palestine to "gain an insight into missionary life and work before she plunged into the responsibilities of housekeeping." She could only visit Cairo for a fortnight in route. Gairdner accepted the postponement, willing, as he put it, to subordinate "our personal desires to the really great end—the good estate of the work." Ultimately, the couple married October 16, 1902, in Nazareth, barely escaping Palestine before a quarantine closed the borders.[11]

Interference in personal matters was only one burden novice missionaries had to bear. Because no one could work in Egypt without a thorough knowledge of Arabic and Islamic society, each newcomer devoted his primary attention to mastering these subjects. The task was exceedingly difficult since the language was complex and instructional techniques were primitive. Gairdner and Thornton studied together "pour[ing] out" their "souls over sounds and guttural letters and grammatical rules." Both men progressed quickly and passed their final examination in November 1901, with Gairdner attaining among the highest scores in mission history.[12]

Even before his studies were complete, Gairdner began his active evangelistic work. His first assignment was superintending the boy's school in Cairo. The task must have been extremely frustrating for an Oxford graduate with an intellectual bent, for the material was elementary and the teachers poorly trained. Gairdner was shocked to discover corruption at this level, with at least one teacher apparently accepting bribes for grades. Nevertheless, class enrollment increased to nearly 100 and the "general efficiency" improved enough for the mission secretary to praise Gairdner's work.

Additional tasks fell to the young Englishman. When most army chaplains in Cairo transferred to South Africa during the Boer War, he held church services for the remaining British troops. He also supervised an Anglican church in Cairo attended by converts and occasionally preached or conducted evangelistic meetings. Gairdner's growing status among his colleagues became evident in November 1902 when he was asked to preside at the mission's annual conference. Two years later he took charge of language training for new missionaries and began improving the syllabus from which they studied.[13]

One factor restricting the development of additional programs was the inavailability of large, well located rooms in which to hold lectures, discussions, and private meetings. Gairdner, Thornton, and mission secretary Adney searched for suitable quarters. Their efforts yielded results in 1902. The building they found had belonged to Ahmed Orabi, the Egyptian rebel whose uprising had resulted in the British occupation of Cairo. Although an "old-fashioned sort of place," by 1913 it had been bought and refurbished to meet the needs of the mission.

Beit Orabi Pasha (Orabi Pasha's house), as the CMS quarters were commonly known, hosted new activities designed to attract progressive, open-minded, educated Moslems. A library offered a variety of reading materials in Arabic and English. Weekly meetings focused on national and social problems; more explicitly evangelistic programs included missionaries speaking on Christian principles, Biblical history, or morality. They caused problems, since Moslems often sat through the proceedings so they could condemn the speakers during the question period afterward. Gairdner regretted the "irritating character" of these sessions, but he realized that they provided the only opportunity to contact these men.[14]

Since most Moslems were reluctant to attend any CMS activity, Gairdner and Thornton suggested issuing a magazine in English and Arabic that could be circulated throughout the country. Its main objective would be promoting Christianity through short articles, Biblical extracts, and other materials "of a definitely religious stamp." Proselyting material would be interspersed with news, discussions of social questions, and announcements of forthcoming activities. As editors, Thornton and Gairdner suggested calling the magazine *Orient and Occident*. The new Cairo mission secretary, Rennie MacInnes, agreed that the magazine would have "a very great influence for good," but he suspected that estimates of cost and time were too low. Receiving the necessary approval and appropriations from London proved difficult, but eventually the CMS authorized a £250 annual subsidy. Gairdner took charge of gathering material, writing articles, and translating them into Arabic. Thornton superintended printing, business arrangements, and circulation.[15]

The first number of *Orient and Occident* appeared in January 1905. Cairo newspapers provided mailing lists so free copies could be mailed throughout Egypt. 1,500 Egyptians, including several hundred Moslems, subscribed. Problems arose in the Sudan when British officials required Moslems to swear that they wished to receive copies before any could be mailed them. Several Arabic newspapers condemned the magazine, and most Cairo street vendors refused to stock it. Still, *O and O* won considerable praise, and it soon became the leading Christian magazine designed for Moslem readers in the Middle East.[16]

The magazine's success stimulated the production of increasing numbers of tracts and booklets. In 1905, just as the first issue appeared, Arthur T. Upson, an experienced English printer, established the inter-denominational Nile Mission Press in Cairo. The number of publications he issued for Moslem readers increased steadily, and by 1919 totaled over 300. Of these more than 40 had been produced by CMS under Gairdner's direct supervision. [17]

Several unexpected events stimulated Gairdner's literary and scholarly activities. The first and most tragic was the sudden death of Douglas Thornton in September 1907 at the age of 34. The two men had worked closely together for more than a decade. The immediate effect was that Gairdner emerged as an independent figure, taking full responsibility for CMS literary activities. To perpetuate the memory of his departed colleague, Gairdner wrote a brief commemorative booklet. A larger full-length biography published in 1907 focused on the successful missionary techniques Thornton had developed.[18]

Gairdner's writing ability impressed CMS officials in London. Early in 1908 General Secretary Baylis asked him to write a lengthy handbook on the Moslem world for use by the Church of England in its home missions program. "You are the right person to undertake the writing of this book, if you will do so," Baylis wrote.[19] Gairdner, flattered by the request, devoted several months to the task. *The Reproach of Islam* outlined the history and beliefs of Mohammedans and explained the problems and opportunities of Christian evangelization. Gairdner enjoyed writing the book. What joy there was, he told friends, to know that one's work would be studied by several thousand "young, intelligent, and ardent readers!"[20]

The book received numerous favorable reviews and went into many additional printings. Years later a list of "best books for the study of Islam" labeled it as "of outstanding importance." "No other small volume," a reviewer of the 1921 reissue noted "gives us a larger amount of well-arranged information on the origin and growth of Islam, its doctrinal teachings and practical effects, and the great task of the Christian church in regard to it."[21]

The book's success prompted requests for Gairdner to undertake additional writing assignments. In 1910 Christian leaders from throughout the world met at Edinburgh for an international missionary conference. They asked Gairdner to spend four or five weeks afterward preparing a volume summarizing the activities of the convention and publicizing its decisions. He devoted the summer to attending the conference and writing the book-length *Echoes from Edinburgh, 1910*. It aimed to make vivid to churchmen, who had been unable to attend, "what the conference really was and did and saw and reached after and believed and hoped."[22] It succeeded admirably, in large measure because of Gairdner's colorful portrayals of the participants, adroit summaries of proceedings, and inspired renderings of the conclusions. "A brilliant literary work," the official CMS historian termed it.[23]

"Ought not Gairdner now to have the chance for studying Islam . . .?" asked Bishop E. G. Ingham during a visit to Cairo in 1910. The Egypt mission badly needed "an authority" on Moslem history, theology, and language. With training available only outside Cairo, Gairdner, the Bishop argued, should become such an expert.[24] Mission Secretary MacInnes endorsed the idea, pointing out Gairdner's qualifications:

> Here is a man [Gairdner] who is probably almost unique in the Mohammedan missions of today, gifted to an extraordinary degree with the power of grasping a subject, probing it, mastering it, then passing on the result of his studies to others, either by means of a fluent and literary pen, or by the inspiration of personal conversation or formal discussion; a man with an already remarkable knowledge of Arabic, and the power of studying the language and literature far more deeply than he has hitherto had the opportunity of doing. . . .[25]

They suggested that Gairdner be given a year's leave for full-time study. Some CMS leaders doubted the value of academic training, but those who contended that increased knowledge would improve the effectiveness of evangelizing work triumphed. Gairdner accepted the offer and pondered how best to spend his time. He decided to visit German universities to work with world renowned Arabists. Then he would cross the Atlantic to study with Professor Duncan MacDonald at Hartford Seminary in Connecticut.[26]

Gairdner called it his "Wanderjahr." In 1910 he moved to Berlin to acquaint himself with important German works on Islam, studying under Professor E. Sachau, a leading authority on Mohammed, attending the famed "Orientalisches Seminar," and visiting missionary training schools. Some of the lectures were disappointingly elementary, but he enjoyed meeting learned professors and perfected his German. In Rotterdam he toured a Dutch missionary college whose "model syllabus and curriculum" might be used in Cairo. He learned about other new methods of teaching Arabic at the Hamburg Colonial Institute. A month in Budapest enabled him to study with Professor I. Goldziher, whom Gairdner termed "the greatest authority on any subject in the world."[27]

The highlight of Gairdner's leave was studying with MacDonald at Hartford Seminary, a small school which specialized in Islamic studies. MacDonald had authored the article on "Allah" in the definitive *Encyclopedia of Islam*; his *Muslim Theology* was the "best general account."[28] Gairdner found him an "enthusiast in his subject and an admirable teacher." The stay was "a complete success." MacDonald introduced him to useful methodological approaches and a vast knowledge of international scholarship. He suggested subjects on which additional research was needed. "To have so many avenues of Arabic and Islamic literature and thought opened to one by such a man," Gairdner concluded, "was a privilege indeed."

Before returning to Cairo, Gairdner immersed himself in the Oriental world. In Aleppo, Syria, he spent a month *incognito*. He lived with a Catholic priest and pretended to be a travelling orientalist. Dressed in *effendi* attire, a tarbush on his head and his feet bared, no one suspecting he was a missionary, Gairdner conversed at length with the leading *sheikhs* of the Levant. "In this way," he later reported, "I could enter more deeply into the Moslem mind and thought than I had ever been able to before."[29]

Gairdner's return in late 1911 initiated a new phase of his career. He was now one of the senior English missionaries in Cairo. Instead of taking orders from superiors, he issued them to his juniors. In 1914, when MacInnes became Anglican bishop in Jerusalem, Gairdner was named Egypt mission secretary. MacInnes also named him Canon of St. George's Collegiate Church in Jerusalem. He seldom visited Palestine and had few duties there, but the title gave him added prestige in church circles.[30]

Gairdner frequently worked with an American missionary and expert on Islam, Samuel M. Zwemer, who moved to Cairo in 1912. Born in Michigan to Dutch Reformed parents, in 1886 he had volunteered for missionary service and four years later went to Arabia, where he established a reputation as a "flaming crusader." He so delighted in handing out tracts in mosques that friends suspected he sought a martyr's end.[31] Gairdner and Zwemer, although differing greatly in background and philosophy, became close friends. When Zwemer founded *The Moslem World*, an international missionary quarterly devoted to the evangelization of Islam, Gairdner became an associate editor.

When missionaries from various churches interested in work among Moslems resolved to establish a "well-equipped college for missionaries to Muslims at Cairo" they charged Gairdner and Zwemer with implementing the proposal. Gairdner dug out his notes on methods used in major European schools and tried to develop an ideal program for Cairo. A meeting of language experts from throughout the Arab world discussed the best instructional methods. Zwemer planned a lecture program in "Islamics." Plans moved rapidly, and the Cairo Study Centre opened in 1913.

In many respects the Centre was a haphazard institution. No permanent classrooms were available, so students congregated wherever they could, often in private homes. There were no full-time instructors. "It is a Study Centre, not a college," reminded the first annual report, "for its superintendents are not professors: They are on the contrary exceedingly busy missionaries with serious responsibilities towards the duties entrusted to them by their societies or churches." Few lectures could be given, and only limited supervision was provided for language instruction. Gairdner took charge of supervising Arabic teaching and located native-speaking instructors, often *sheikhs* trained at Al-Azhar University. During the first five years, the Centre attracted about fifty students, more than half from the British or American missions, but including workers from India, Norway, Sweden, and Syria as well.[32]

Existing teaching materials failed to meet the needs of foreigners desiring to learn Arabic quickly, so, using the methods and linguistic knowledge he had acquired in Europe and America, Gairdner wrote a text for the Study Centre. It used an international phonetic script so students could learn the spoken language directly; teachers helped develop a series of modern and natural dialogues suited to missionary needs. *Egyptian Colloquial Arabic: A Conversational Grammar* appeared through an English press in 1917. Reviewers greeted its publication with acclaim, noting that it was the first "reform" text for Arabic or any other semitic or oriental language. "It means much, therefore," W. H. Worrell noted, "both for Arabic studies and phonetic studies. . . ."[33]

The Study Centre's other problems required outside assistance. American missionary Earl Elder relieved Gairdner of some responsibilities by supervising day-to-day activities. After the American University at Cairo opened in 1920, its president, Charles R. Watson, volunteered to take over the Centre. "Under the University it would be possible," he explained "to give greater stability to this important work, to equip it more fully, to give it a permanent domicile, and finally, to extend its services to a still wider circle." Final arrangements were soon completed, and the new School of Oriental Studies opened in the fall of 1921. Gairdner's relationship with the institution continued, but especially after the arrival of Australian Arabist Arthur Jeffrey he had little to do with administration.[34]

Gairdner enhanced his reputation as an Arabic scholar by producing a series of important publications. In some, such as a description of Al-Azhar, he explained Islamic institutions and beliefs to European Christians. His translation of Al-Ghazzali's *The Niche of Lights* made an important work by an 11th century scholastic available to English readers. Gairdner became interested in Islamic mysticism and interviewed several Sufis to understand their beliefs better.[35] He studied the life of the Prophet Mohammed. His brief biography "without camouflage" argued that Mohammed was a man of his time who committed wrongs and made mistakes. He could not provide the kinds of moral examples Christ did for Christians. Often, too, Gairdner's book examined the differences between Islamic and Christian beliefs or compared descriptions of the same event in the Bible and Koran. Moslems, who emphasized the unity of God, found the Christian concept of the Trinity perplexing, so Gairdner prepared a series of lengthy articles which missionaries could use to explain and defend the concept. An article called on churches to develop a plan for helping new members.[36] In addition to these major writings, he prepared a regular column for *Moslem World*, reviewed books for a number of publications, and continued to edit *Orient and Occident*.

As the senior English missionary in Cairo after 1914, he found time to enjoy many of the artistic interests born in his youth. A talented musician, he often played the piano or organ, and at missionary conferences frequently selected and led the singing. "Of all men and women," John Mott recalled, "no one has ever surpassed Canon Gairdner of Cairo in his inspired intuition as to the hymn and the time that would be most helpful at a given moment." Studies of Arabic musical traditions enabled him to write Christian hymns that would appeal to oriental listeners.[37] He loved the theater, and his home was often the scene of dramatic readings, which delighted friends. His portrayals of Charlie Chaplain brought "uproarious amusement" to children and adults. His own play, *Joseph and His Brothers*, played before appreciative audiences in Cairo. After 1921, when it was published in Britain and America, the play became a mainstay in the repertoire of missions throughout the world.[38]

Gairdner also established a reputation for being colorful, sometimes eccentric. He was a common sight on the Cairo streets as he peddled his bicycle to or from some engagement. He was notoriously absent-minded, and sometimes his colleagues worried about his inability to manage his own affairs. His clothing was frequently poorly fitting and mis-matched. "He was too busy about men's souls," Zwemer explains, "to spend much time on dress." Once when leaving for an extended visit to Scotland, he left his bicycle with the Cairo station porter as though he were to be gone only a few days. His friends, who found this unsurprising, were astonished that he remembered to claim it when he returned.[39]

Despite his many interests, Gairdner found it difficult to escape the heavy demands of missionary life. As Secretary of the Egypt mission, he supervised dozens of missionaries, presided at meetings, corresponded with CMS officials, and attended many social functions. Evangelization was always his first obligation, and he preached, conducted meetings for non-Christian inquirers, or counseled individual converts. He was active in the Cairo branch of the YMCA. When a CMS employee rejected Christianity, secretly returning to Islam, Gairdner spent several months finding the man, persuading him of his error, and attempting to repair the damage. During World War I the fighting in Palestine, the presence of thousands of British and Australian troops in Cairo, and the difficulties in communicating with London put additional burdens on the reduced and overworked CMS staff.[40]

After the War the changing political situation in Egypt forced Gairdner to adjust the goals and objectives of his mission. As nationalism intensified, foreigners, especially missionaries, encountered new obstacles in conducting their work; a strong, well financed movement among Moslems countered the efforts of Christians and attempted to "remove the doubts of the people concerning Islam, and to demonstrate its truths." The British ended their protectorate in 1922, although continuing to control the Suez Canal and maintain troops in other parts of the country.

Because of such changes, few programs Gairdner had originated retained their effectiveness. For example, the CMS had established churches for its converts, but they were administered through the mission and served by English pastors. The church hierarchy was entirely foreign. Gairdner hoped that all Christians — Egyptian and English — could find a "spiritual home" on the same locally-oriented churches. To encourage the development of an Egyptian Anglican congregation, in 1925 he helped organize the "Episcopal Church in Egypt in Communion with the Church of England." Native clergymen were ordained, and the local church assumed many responsibilities previously born by the English mission.[41]

Factionalism consistently hindered the work of Christians. Protestant missionaries from different sects or nations as often squabbled among themselves as with Moslems. In 1920 to encourage friendlier relations and foster co-operation Gairdner and other leading missionaries founded the Egypt Inter-Mission Council. Some sects refused to join, but regular meetings and unified policies significantly reduced counterproductive competition. The following year a more comprehensive group, the Fellowship of Unity, organized the Greek Orthodox, Coptic, Armenian, Evangelical (Protestant), and Anglican churches. The preparation and distribution of material for Moslems was also co-ordinated.[42]

Gairdner's numerous missionary, scholarly, cultural, and administrative activities inevitably strained his fragile health. Late in 1927, when he developed a fever, doctors found that his lungs had become abscessed, probably from tuberculosis. The illness did not disrupt a full Christmas holiday schedule. The fever soon worsened, however, and by early 1928 he turned over much responsibility to others. Gairdner proved "always patient and uncomplaining" during his "suffering and weakness." On May 23, 1928, he died at the age of 54. The funeral at the CMS cemetery in Old Cairo was attended by hundreds of friends, including many Egyptians, some Moslem. The crowd, reported *The Times*, "afforded elegant testimony to the place which Canon Gairdner [had] gained among the Moslem as well as among the Christian community in Egypt."[43]

Spanning more than a quarter century, Gairdner's career in many ways exemplified the role of English missionaries throughout the world. He sometimes exuded the over-confidence, self-righteousness, arrogance, and naivete associated with imperialism. He believed, as did millions of others, that the Empire could became modern only if it became European and Christian. As a young missionary he knew little and cared less about Egypt's traditions and culture. He obediently accepted the rules and bureaucracy of the Christian missionary community.

Unlike some of his colleagues, Gairdner altered his views. Through study he came to appreciate the subtleties, beauty, and complexity of the local language. Knowledge of history, theology, literature, and music gave him uncommon insight into a rich culture. Ultimately, Middle Eastern society may well have affected him as much as he altered it.

Indeed, by any reasonable standard, Gairdner and his coworkers had little impact on the religious life of Egypt. The CMS baptized an average of about twenty Moslems a year. The percentage of Christians in Egypt barely increased.[44] In broader perspective, however, men like Gairdner, together with government and private agencies, helped prepare countries like Egypt for modernization. Through their efforts citizens learned about Western ideas. The whole society became less tradition-bound. New concepts and methods were more welcome. National leaders sought increasingly to introduce modern developments into their countries.

Missionaries were also important in increasing Western academic and popular interest in the non-Western world. Christians often began by learning a language so they could deal with potential converts. Many developed long-term professional interests in the area. A few became authorities on Moslem theology, language, or literature. Their writings informed readers in Europe or America about the Middle East. Eventually a corps of experts developed, and interested readers became better informed about what had once been a mysterious part of the world.

Notes

1. James Quay interviewed by the author February 1, 1973.
2. Constance E. Padwick, *Temple Gairdner of Cairo* (London: Society for Promoting Christian Knowledge, 1929), pp. 3-14.
3. Samuel M. Zwemer, "Canon W. H. T. Gairdner of Cairo," *Missionary Review of the World* 12 (February 1929), 14-16.
4. J. C. Pollock, *A Cambridge Movement* (London: John Murray, 1953), pp. 54-137 *passim*; W. H. T. Gairdner, *D. M. Thornton: A Study in Missionary Ideals and Methods* (London: Hodder & Stoughton, 1908), pp. 17-61.
5. *The Times* (London), May 23, 1928, p. 21. Thornton, "Report on Efforts to reach young men of Cairo," 1904, Church Missionary Society, Egypt Mission letters, Center for Research Libraries, Chicago [hereinafter cited as CMSECRL], roll 222.
6. Eugene Stock, *The History of the Church Missionary Society* (London: CMS, 1899) 1:227, 350-51; 3: 514-15, 745-50. James T. Addison, *The Christian Approach to the Moslem: A Historical Study* (New York: Columbia University Press, 1942), pp. 141-45. H. E. Fox, "Instructions . . . autumn of 1897." CMSECRL, roll 217.
7. Gairdner, *Thornton*, p. 63.
8. Thornton, "Report on Efforts to reach young men of Cairo," 1904, CMSECRL, roll 222.
9. "Instructions . . . to Mr. W. H. T. Gairdner," October 6, 1899, CMSECRL, roll 217.
10. F. F. Adney to F. Baylis, October 12, 1901, CMSECRL, roll 217. Padwick, *Gairdner*, pp. 88-90.
11. Correspondence related to the controversy is in CMSECRL, rolls 217 and 221.
12. Gairdner, *Thornton*, 75; Thornton to Baylis, June 9, 1901; and results of language examinations November 1901, CMSECRL, roll 221.
13. Annual report, CMS Mission, Egypt, 1901 & 1902; Minutes, Egypt Mission annual conference, 1901 & 1903, CMSECRL, roll 221.
14. Adney to Gladstone, December 5, 1902; Gairdner, "Circular Letter to Friends, No. II," (printed), June 25, 1903, both in CMSECRL, roll 221. Gairdner, *Thornton*, p. 155 ff.
15. Minutes, Egypt Mission conference, 1905; MacInnes to Baylis, May 9, 1904, Thornton to Pendry, November 29, 1905, CMSECRL, roll 222. Gairdner, *Thornton*, p. 207. Arthur T. Upson, "The Need for Arabic Christian Literature," *The Moslem World*, 10 (January 1919), 44.

16. Thornton to Stock, January 8, 1905; Gairdner to "Dear Friends," (printed), August 5, 1905; *Cairene and Fallaheen*, No. 3 (Cairo: Nile Mission Press, 1907), p. 9-10 CMSECRL, roll 222.
17. Upson, "Arabic Christian Literature," pp. 44-45.
18. Gairdner, *Douglas Montagu Thornton* (Cairo: Nile Mission Press, 1907).
19. Baylis to Gairdner, January 15, 1908; Gairdner to "My Dear Friends," (printed), September 13, 1908, and January 1909, CMSECRL, roll 223.
20. Gairdner to "My Dear Friends," (printed), January 1909, CMSECRL, roll 223.
21. *The Missionary Review of the World* 45 (May 1922), 416. Ernest W. Riggs, "Best Books for the Study of Islam," *The Missionary Review of the World* 49 (October 1926), 829-30.
22. Oldham to H. E. Fox, February 24, 1910 CMSECRL, roll 223; Baylis to Gairdner, March 11, 1910, CMSECRL, roll 218. Gairdner, *Echoes from Edinburgh, 1910* (New York: Fleming H. Revell & Co., 1910), pp. v-vi.
23. Eugene Stock, *The History of the Church Missionary Society: Supplementary Volume* (London: CMS, 1916), pp. 110, 115, 560.
24. Ingham, "journal" with covering letter dated April 19, 1910, CMSECRL, roll 223.
25. MacInnes to Baylis, April 7, 1910, CMSECRL, roll 223.
26. Gairdner, "Annual Report, January 1912," CMSECRL, roll 224.
27. Ibid. Gairdner, "Report," November 20, 1910, CMSECRL, roll 224. Gairdner, "A Missionary's 'Wanderjahr,'" *The Church Missionary Review*, 63 (August 1911), 491-93.
28. Claude Cahen, ed., *Jean Sauvaget's Introduction to the History of the Muslim East: A Biographical Guide* (Berkeley: University of California Press, 1965), 98, *The Moslem World* 2 (July 1912), 312-17.
29. Gairdner, "Annual Report," January 1912, CMSECRL, roll 224.
30. G. R. Mauley to R. F. McNeile, October 3, 1914, CMSECRL, roll 218. Stock, *Church Missionary Society: Supplementary Volume*, p. 113.
31. Sherwood Eddy, *Pathfinders of the World Missionary Crusade* (London: Whitmore and Stone, 1945), pp. 240-45.
32. E. M. Wherry, G. C. Mylrea, and S. M. Zwemer, eds., *Lucknow, 1911* (London: Christian Literature Society for India, 1911), pp. 38, 45-72. Gairdner, "Missionary Training Methods on the Continent," 1911; Gairdner to "My Dear Friends," (printed), June 1912; and "*Prospectus of the Study Centre for Arabic and Islam in Cairo* (Cairo: n.p., 1912), CMSECRL, roll 224. *The Moslem World* 4 (January 1914), 96-7; 8 (April 1918), 202-03; 12 (October, 1922), 390-9.
33. Gairdner, *Egyptian Colloquial Arabic: A Conversational Grammar*

(Cambridge: W. Hefer & Sons., 1917); *The Moslem World*, 8 (January 1918), 84-88.

34. American University at Cairo, *Special News Bulletin*, February 14, 1921, 6. C. P. Russell to Watson, March 1, 1921, and Zwemer to Watson, March 1, 1921, Archives, American University in Cairo. *The United Presbyterian*, 81 (January 25, 1923), 12-13.
35. Gairdner, "El-Azhar Collegiate-Mosque and the Mohammedan Propaganda," *The East and the West* 9 (July 1911), 256-73; Gairdner, trans., Al-Ghazzali, *Miskhat Al-Anwar (The Niche of Lights)*, (London: Royal Asiatic Society, 1924); Gairdner, "'The Way' of a Mohammedan Mystic," *The Moslem World* 2 (1912), 171-91, 245-57.
36. Gairdner, "Mohammed Without Camouflage: Ecce Homo Aribacus," *The Moslem World* 9 (1919), 25-57; "Mohammedan Tradition and Gospel Record," *The Moslem World* 5 (October 1915), 349-79; "The Doctrine of the Unity in Trinity," *The Moslem World* 5 (October 1915), 381-407; 6 (1916), 28-41, 127-39; "The Christian Church as a Home for Christ's Converts from Islam," *The Moslem World*, 14 (July 1924), 235-46.
37. Zwemer, "Gairdner," 92; Basil Mathews, *John R. Mott: World Citizen* (New York and London: Harper and Brothers, 1934), 329. Gairdner, "The Vital Force of the Chanting of the Koran in the Devotional Life of the Moslem," in S. M. Zwemer, ed., *The Vital Forces of Christianity and Islam* (London: Oxford University Press, 1915). Gairdner, "The Source and Character of Oriental Music," *The Moslem World* 6 (October 1916), 347-56.
38. Zwemer, "Gairdner," 95-6; Gairdner, *Joseph and His Brothers* (London: Society for Promoting Christian Knowledge, 1921).
39. Zwemer, "Gairdner," 92; Eddy, *Pathfinders*, p. 247.
40. Padwick, *Temple Gairdner*, pp. 241-50.
41. *The Moslem World*, 1 (1911), 187-90, 439-42. Addison, *Christian Approach*, pp. 148-49. Padwick, *Temple Gairdner*, pp. 263-64, 269-74.
42. Ibid., pp. 265-69. Addision, *Christian Approach*, pp. 168-69.
43. Margaret D. Gairdner, "Dear Friends, Both His and Mine," June 14, 1928 (printed), Archives, American University in Cairo. *The Times* (London), May 23, 1928, p. 21.
44. Kenneth Scott Latourette, *Advance Through Storm* (New York: Harper and Row, 1945), pp. 258-59.

8

Lord Robert Cecil: Apostle of the League

by
Jere Langdon Jackson
Stephen F. Austin State University

On December 20, 1920 as the First Assembly of the League of Nations ended its sessions, *The Times*, in an editorial entitled the "League's Hopeful Beginning," referred to Lord Robert Cecil as

> the apostle of the League, whose personality, full of spiritual fervour, has again and again brought into the debate at the right moment the larger atmosphere of conciliation without which the many conflicting interests represented might have seriously impaired its harmony.[1]

Reflecting on those hopeful days, Professor Gilbert Murray in 1948 listed several "if's" or slight changes that he thought might have altered the course of history in the interwar years: "If at the first start, in the early twenties, we had had in the Foreign Office a statesman like Grey or Cecil, who understood and cared for the League, instead of Lord Curzon, who was steeped in the old diplomatic tradition . . ."[2] While it is quite possible that no individual could have come to terms with the forces at work after World War I, some speculation along the lines suggested by Murray provides a useful device for examining at least one of the major problems of the early twenties: namely, the death of ideas.

Why, one might ask, study "failures" like the League of Nations or Lord Robert Cecil? While historians will no doubt continue to debate the good and the bad effects that both the League and Cecil had on policy, those who ignore the institution or the man simply because they were not ultimately successful do so at their own peril and to the distortion of history. As for the soundness of a biographical approach to any subject, Charles F. Mullett's statement in *Biography as History* seems appropriate:

> First and last history is about people, what they do, what they think, what happens to them, and how they influence the world in which they live. No matter the attention to deeds, institutions, and ideas, the historian comes back to the men who performed the deeds, ran the institutions, and conceived the ideas.[3]

Moreover, since Lord Robert's approach to the problems of the early twenties was so different from that of Lord Curzon, the question raised by Murray—whether Britain could have used the League as a more effective instrument of policy—certainly seems pertinent.

In retrospect, the central question that plagued British leaders in the inter-war years, and which, with some new twists, continued to plague them after World War II, was this: to what extent is Britain a part of Europe? For those who argued that she was an integral part, the problem became the extent of her responsibility in the creation of European economic and political security. For isolationists, the problem became the extent to which Britain could remain detached without endangering her own economic and political security.

Professor W. N. Medlicott argues that Britain's successive attempts to respond to both her problems and the realitites of the modern world were complicated and delayed by strong internal forces of public opinion that pushed the country into a new and unaccustomed role of international leadership.[4] In particular, he singles out the League of Nations movement as instrumental in preventing realistic adjustments. Since many authorities would agree with Medlicott that Britain's resources were not equal to the role in world affairs that she was expected to fill, the question arises, how well did her leaders marshall the resources at their disposal? On this point, Professor F. S. Northedge goes further than Medlicott:

> The failure of British policy between the two wars was indeed a failure of resources; but it was more truly a failure of ideas, or rather a failure to adjust ideas born in one age to the requirements of another.[5]

The essential truth of this conclusion should be obvious to those who have seriously studied British diplomacy in this period; its tragedy, however, only becomes poignant if one looks at the early twenties when there was still flexibility.

Between 1919 and 1924, when faced with a movement on the part of British officials to abandon completely the security provisions of the Covenant of the League of Nations and at the same time reject further commitments on the European continent, Lord Robert Cecil, almost single-handedly and without any official status, checked the drift of British policy back into the pre-war mold of isolation. On almost every major foreign policy issue of the day he put forth elaborate and alternative suggestions to official policy. Many of his ideas came to be summarized in the so-called Draft Treaty of Mutual Assistance. While Conservatives and Labour leaders alike rejected both Cecil's ideas and his Draft Treaty, eventually, as Cecil noted in his diary, they "found it impossible to persist in a purely negative attitude."[6] They had to supply answers to the questions he raised. They did so by adopting, in modified and incomplete form, Cecil's solutions. Labour's Geneva Protocol in 1924 and the Locarno Treaties negotiated by the Conservatives in 1925 drew heavily on Cecil's briefs. Significantly, these ideas did initiate a new and more hopeful era in European affairs. What if Cecil had been the Foreign Secretary between 1919 and 1924? What if his ideas, proposed in detail early in the twenties, had been given a fair hearing before the Ruhr invasion or the Corfu Incident?

It is the thesis of this essay that the real delinquents of the inter-war years, especially in the twenties, were the "escapists" of both the left and the right. The pacifists of the left hid their heads in the sand and refused to believe that policemen are as necessary to society as respect for the law. The so-called realists of the right, when faced with the sudden necessity of great change of habit and outlook, refused to contemplate new solutions to new problems because these solutions interfered with old prejudices. The "escapists" refused to recognize that statesmanship, especially in the inter-war years, involved a mixture of a readiness to wage war and a determination to maintain peace. Certainly, Robert Cecil did recognize this necessary balance and perceived the League as a method of maintaining it.

Edgar Algernon Robert Gascoyne-Cecil was born in 1864 at the height of the Victorian Age. Great Britain at the time was prosperous, secure, self-confident, the acknowledged leader of the world powers. Lord Robert's personal circumstances were as propitious as the conditions of the country. As the son of the third Marquess of Salisbury, the leading Conservative peer in England, he was born into the ruling elite.[7]

In his autobiography, Cecil divided his public life into three phases: his professional career as a barrister, his work for the Conservative Party, and his "absorption in efforts for maintenance of peace."[8] His transition from barrister to politician took place around the turn of the century against a backdrop of fundamental national changes and traumatic personal readjustments. Because of the position of his family in the establishment, he looked upon change as a personal affront. Therefore, after his first election to Parliament in 1906, he became a very effective guerilla fighter against the social and economic programs of the Liberal government. The third phase of his career, his work for the League of Nations, began in 1916 and lasted until 1946.

To attribute Cecil's intellectual disposition toward order in international affairs solely to his experiences during the First World War would be an oversimplification. In practical terms, however, the creative force behind his commitment to the League of Nations stemmed from his passionate hatred of the disorder he witnessed after 1914. It was the war itself, with its barbarism and almost total destruction of morality especially religious values, that pushed Cecil into a search for an alternative to war as a means of settling international disputes. It is significant that Cecil wrote his first memorandum on the League in 1916 while serving as Minister of Blockade, the central figure in Britain's economic war against Germany. His need for the League was as much psychological as it was rational; he had to have something positive and idealistic. Cecil was actually to become something of a fanatic on the subject. As such, he shared with the infamous men of the inter-war years a certain revolutionary mentality, albeit the direction of his revolutionary activity was not one normally associated with the violent years after the war. Cecil's obsession was for a more rationally organized world where international rivalries were at least partially harnessed; men like Hitler and Mussolini welcomed struggle, Cecil spent his every energy trying to control it.

Although A. J. P. Taylor irreverently called Cecil one of "the hot-gospellers of the Covenant," he also noted something about Cecil frequently overlooked by other historians: namely, that Cecil was primarily a system-maker.[9] He concerned himself with means and methods as well as ends. He sought to institutionalize the means whereby international politics could be tamed and channeled for the benefit of humanity. In his work opposite President Woodrow Wilson on the League Commission in 1919 and later as the guiding spirit at the first Assemblies of the League, Cecil proved this. In addition, despite his aristocratic background, he was a democratic statesman. He came to advocate in the years after the war "participatory democracy" in both foreign and domestic affairs. He took the public into his confidence and treated them in a straightforward, honest manner. He believed in the public's ability to make sound decisions, provided they were given adequate information, honest leadership, and sufficient time.[10]

Physically, Lord Robert was a striking figure — six feet four inches tall. The American ambassador to Britain during the First World War described him as "tall, lank, and ungainly, almost Lincolnesque in the carelessness of his apparel and the exceeding awkwardness of his posture and manners."[11] In personal habits he was conservative like his father. He never spoke flippantly or superficially. If, on rare occasions, he proved witty, it no doubt surprised him as much as his audience. He was courteous, patient, scrupulously honest, and above all sincere. His instinct at any given moment was to try to do what he thought was morally right, whether possible or not, regardless of what it did to his political interests.

Nature endowed Lord Robert with admirable personal qualities. He possessed a fine intellect and a good memory. His genius was for hard work, quietly done. Colonel Edward House has written one of the most cogent character sketches of him:

> With a character of almost austere simplicity he had a win-

> ning charm of manner, and the force which was behind his observations rested largely upon his almost incredible frankness and his obvious sincerity. His mental attitude is an extraordinary combination of the conservative, the practical, and the idealistic.[12]

If he were alive today, Lord Robert would be described as committed. He believed deeply and sincerely in all of his causes, the majority of which were good. His willpower, his courage in independent action, and his integrity of purpose made him a formidable opponent and a useful ally. When Cecil thought the government was wrong, he was willing to resign. Had he subordinated his principles now and then to the needs of the moment, he might have been a more successful politician and more venerated by historians as a greater statesman. One of his associates summed up his character by saying, "He was nearly a great man, and he was certainly a good man; possibly as great a man as so good a man can be."[13]

Robert Cecil, stripped of the myths in which his supporters and opponents have clothed him, proved to be neither a knight coming to save the new world from the old nor a naive devotee of unrealistic internationalism. After careful study, he emerges as a practical man concerned with long-range problems, one who brought to these problems an extraordinary foresight and depth of understanding. Cecil thought Europe's sacrifices would eventually have to be repeated unless she utilized the period of exhaustion following the war to build up machinery against future disturbances. Inaction, therefore, was a crime. Problems did not go away if they were ignored. Cecil came to believe that use of the wrong methods might also compromise peace. What was needed was an "offensive-defensive."[14] To trust the maintenance of peace simply to the healing influences of time, he told Ramsey MacDonald, was "indefensively optimistic."[15]

In the years immediately following the Versailles Conference, Lord Robert became Lloyd George's leading critic in foreign affairs. Cecil was the first of the Prime Minister's inner circle to warn the public of the latter's unreliable diplomatic methods. Cecil saw in Lloyd George's showy, ill-prepared diplomacy the seeds of future distrust and suspicion. Between 1919 and 1922,

Cecil mercilessly pointed out the dangers of the Prime Minister's duplicity, ambiguity, and vacillation; he laid bare the divisions in the Cabinet and the weaknesses of the Foreign Office *vis à vis* Downing Street. He warned the public of the unsettling effects that continued improvisation would have on the country's prestige abroad.[16] Cecil, of course, hoped to alert Conservatives by his exposures. Because he linked his criticisms with an advocacy of the League of Nations, they ignored his analysis.[17]

While modern authors concede the correctness of Cecil's criticisms of Lloyd George's diplomatic methods,[18] one cannot help but lament the breakdown in cooperation between these two men. An alliance between them might have substantially improved the League's chances of success and thereby served well the interests of peace. Both men were activists. Lloyd George was a dynamic leader with political *savoir faire*. Cecil, to quote one of his associates, not only "embodied the nature, experience, and traditional wisdom of statesmanship," but he also possessed "a rare combination of the practical and the ideal in his thinking."[19] Cecil had charisma as well as character. After witnessing the way Lord Robert had "from the first to last dominated the [First] Assembly," the *Manchester Guardian* warned that nothing would "be more foolish than to underrate the power of a single vigorous personality directed with perfect disinterestedness to just ends."[20] As to Cecil's ability to create public opinion, within a few years he turned the League of Nations Union into, what D. C. Watts has termed, "the single most important and influential pressure group in British foreign politics between the wars."[21]

Lloyd George was an "escapist" in the sense that he refused to do anything politically courageous. Many of his proposals for the pacification of Europe were perfectly legitimate. He was usually willing to select an enlightened alternative if given the politically safe opportunity to do so. During the war and the peace conference, Lloyd George allowed Cecil to strengthen his own natural inclinations by providing practical, yet enlightened alternatives, as long as Cecil did the fighting. The Prime Minister frequently needed an opening to the left, someone who could beat down the more imperialistic and reactionary elements with the coalition.[22] Cecil, understandably, tired of the Prime Minister's opportunism. Yet, if he could have looked upon the Prime Minister as the morally neutral force that he was, the men could have made a tremendously positive impact on the post-war world. As it turned out, Cecil abandoned the Prime Minister either to advisers like Lord Curzon and Arthur Balfour who epitomized the older order diplomatically or to adventurers like Winston Churchill. Cecil also took the League into opposition with him; Lloyd George's continual use of conference diplomacy and his reliance upon Lord Curzon was in large part his answer to Cecil's demand for a new form of diplomacy.

It would be unfair to blame Lord Curzon for the confused state of Britain's foreign policy between 1919 and 1922. He suffered a nightmare of abuses under Lloyd George. When freed from this and when dealing with his own speciality—the East—as he was during the Lausanne Conference in 1922, Curzon proved he could conduct an effective foreign policy. Curzon's methods were not as faulty as those of Lloyd George. What Curzon lacked was a sense of proportion and vision. He consistently sacrificed principle to expediency, the long-range to the short. Equally disturbing considering the problems facing him, he did not understand or care deeply for European problems.[23] Nowhere did these faults become more evident than in his relations with France and Italy.

According to his biographer, Curzon accepted "the inevitability, in all human affairs, of competition, combativeness and hostility; and as a corollary of this . . . suspicion of all gestures of conciliation."[24] Curzon's anti-French biases, born during his service in the East and fed by his conception of competitive nationalism, prevented him from seeing the deeper security needs of France. Curzon knew how to deal with intransigent French politicians; what he failed to understand was why the French kept such leaders in office. Consequently, he never really rose above Lloyd George's tactic of alternating between conciliatory and belligerent attitudes toward France.

Lord Robert's sense of proportion, in contrast to Curzon's, was sound, and his understanding of European problems remarkable. Cecil knew that if Europe were ever to experience any real peace his own country would have to abandon isolation and accept its position as a part of Europe and as a producer of security there.[25] In 1919, after the American refusal to enter the League, Cecil watched with alarm as British leaders began to retreat into isolationism. He did what he could in Parliament and in Geneva to counter this.[26] In 1921, when the retreat took the form of undermining the security provisions of the Covenant's Articles 10 and 16, Cecil was horrified. He viewed the attempt to withdraw from the sanction articles as irresponsible and certainly unfair to the French. Although at the time Cecil was pressing for disarmament through the League, he realized and admitted before the entire Assembly that France and every other country had a right to expect security before agreeing to disarmament.[27] Consequently, Cecil had to abate his demands for disarmament in order to rebuild the structure of collective security undermined by officials in London and to prevent any further attempts by his country to withdraw from European problems. A plan was needed, he told Leon Bourgeois, "which would give real security not only to France but to all nations of Europe."[28]

Although at the time serving in Geneva only as the second delegate from South Africa, Cecil had established for himself a commanding position in the League. Using the forum of the League's Temporary Mixed Commission for Disarmament, on which he sat as a private citizen, Cecil attempted to establish the basic premise in the minds of members that security and disarmament were indissolubly linked. Since there were gaps in the security provisions, Cecil called for the drafting of a treaty of mutual guarantee dependent upon the acceptance of a general plan for disarmament. Cecil's proposals in the form passed by the Third Assembly, came to be known as Resolution XIV.[29] The British response was lukewarm. The French, however, said they were "in the strange position of being more anxious for Lord Robert Cecil's plan to succeed than Lord Robert Cecil was himself."[30] Had British leaders in 1922 given any indication that they sincerely understood French security needs, would the French have acted as they did in the Ruhr? Probably not. They were begging for some sign that Britain cared.[31]

Cecil submitted his first draft of a treaty based on Resolution XIV in December of 1922. Throughout 1923, he negotiated to make it acceptable to as many views as possible without destroying its integrity. In the incredibly tangled Fourth Assembly, Cecil piloted his treaty through "without important changes."[32] It was a remarkable document. First, it strengthened the Council by giving it broad powers of inquiry to designate an aggressor in case of hostilities. Second, it made the application of economic and military sanctions automatic and binding once the Council invoked them. Third, the Council could call for military support from the signatory powers; it could organize and transport troops, furnish financial aid to victims of aggression, appoint commanders, assign reparations, and approve any regional arrangement necessary to supplement the general guarantee. The obligations of the treaty were limited to one's own continent, however. Fourth, the entire scheme was made dependent on the general acceptance of a plan for the reduction and limitation of armaments to be drawn up by the Council. One authority has since called it, "the one and only bold approach that the League . . . ever made towards an effective system of mutual assistance." Cecil's Draft Treaty of Mutual Assistance "contained nearly all the essential elements of the [United Nations] system which was eventually adopted at San Francisco."[33]

Cecil's belief that the League would work if the British supported it proved to be correct when he finally got his chance to represent the country in the summer of 1923. He proved he could use the Council as an effective instrument of foreign policy. In July of 1923, Cecil conducted a very difficult inquiry into the problems of the Saar Territory without alienating the French. To quote the somewhat surprised Foreign Office official who had been assigned to keep Cecil in line, Lord Robert "showed firmness and at the same time an extremely conciliatory disposition."[34] Even Curzon felt obliged to congratulate Cecil "on the admirable tact and judgment" he had used in Geneva.[35] Nevertheless, because of Curzon's presence as Foreign Secretary, any creative use of the League as an instrument of British foreign policy had to wait until the advent of a Labour Government in 1924, which utilized in large part, the policies outlined and disseminated by Lord Robert and the League of Nations Union. For instance, Cecil's proposals for a settlement of the Ruhr Crisis, which Curzon rather brusquely suppressed in favor of his own truculent note of August 10, 1923, were very similar to those used by Labour in 1924 and the Conservatives in 1925. Cecil's proposals were firm, yet conciliatory, and linked the whole pacification of Europe into his general efforts to secure disarmament through some supplemental form of security and the entrance of Germany into the League.[36] As Frank Walters has written, Cecil's initiative in 1922 proved "the starting-point of all subsequent attempts . . . Resolution XIV of 1922 led on to the Treaty of Mutual Assistance . . . , to the Geneva Protocol of 1924, and to the Locarno Treaties of 1925."[37]

Traditionally, Cecil has been pictured as the uncompromising supporter of League prerogatives.[38] British documents for the period reveal him to be much more sophisticated in his use of the League than originally thought. He proved conclusively in the Corfu Incident that he understood completely the usefulness of the League in a crisis. He did intend to deny Mussolini the fruits of aggression and stood ready to use all of the machinery of the League, even economic sanctions. Nevertheless, he, perhaps more than anyone, knew the weaknesses of the Covenant; he wanted to close the gaps. Cecil worked creatively and skillfully to get the Corfu crisis settled at the lower level of the Conference of Ambassadors, all the time orchestrating the moral force of public opinion in Geneva by threatening League action. Even Mussolini knew the truth of the American Ambassador's remark on September 21, 1923: "It was apparent at every moment that fear of something occurring at Geneva was the driving power [for a settlement]."[39] It was Cecil's control of this machinery that was impressive. Had he not been undercut at every hand by the British Ambassador in Paris and by Lord Curzon in London, the outcome of the entire incident might have been quite different and more favorable to the League.

Curzon failed to see that a man like Mussolini might eventually threaten everyone's security. For personal reasons, he suppressed the papers that would have vindicated British actions during the crisis; the documents reveal Curzon's mismanagement, vacillation, and unwarranted appeasement.[40] It was not the League's failure, but rather Curzon's shift from reluctant appeasement during the crisis to active courtship of Mussolini in October, November, and December of 1923 that encouraged the Italian to new adventures.[41] By the autumn of that year, Curzon's policy toward the French had collapsed, and the Foreign Secretary was willing to pay almost any price for Mussolini's aid in preventing France from carving up Germany.

Personally, Curzon was to pay a heavy price for his capitulation in the Corfu matter. It cost him the Foreign Office in the Second Baldwin Government. "That nemesis," his biographer wrote,

> which waits on those who show weakness in high places was not slow to impose on Curzon a penalty for this vacillation. His hesitation over the Corfu incident not only damaged our prestige in Europe and the world, but weakened Curzon's own authority in the Cabinet.[42]

Curzon was in many ways typical of Conservative opinion. The Conservatives wanted to limit or suppress the League, not because they were against the use of armed force, but because they felt the League limited Britain's independence, forced her out of her traditional isolation, cut across her imperial ties, and obliged her to take too active a role in European affairs.[43] Many of these same arguments were used in the 1950's to avoid the Common Market.

Labourites opposed the League, in part, for opposite reasons—it had coercive elements. In the period from 1919 to 1923, Cecil had to defend the League from both left and right! By 1923, however, a group of Labourites, led by Arthur Henderson, J. H. Thomas, and J. R. Clynes, had gradually come into close cooperation with Cecil.[44] MacDonald resented Cecil's challenge to his leadership and influence over policy. He even published a warning to Labour not "to become the mere catspaws of the League's devotees, and do nothing except through the League."[45] MacDonald also accused Norman Angell of being "hypnotized by Bob Cecil and his Treaty of Mutual Assistance."[46] When it came time for MacDonald to consider the Draft Treaty, he joined with the permanent officials, who used the arguments of the Conservatives, to reject Cecil's ideas. Nevertheless, after he decided to go to Geneva for the Fifth Assembly, he carefully analyzed the questions that Cecil had outlined. Then, MacDonald helped create a plan, the Geneva Protocol, which was virtually identical to Cecil's excepting its emphasis on arbitration as the vital link in the equation of disarmament and collective security. Labour in 1924 became officially committed to the League and to collective security, but the pacifist wing never took the need for organizing military force to protect peace seriously until after World War II when they entered the United Nations and NATO. MacDonald said,

> my protection really is, not that there is organized force around me, but that there are involuntary social habits around me . . . It is not so much the policemen that one depends on as public opinion.[48]

President Woodrow Wilson is rightfully considered the "Father of the League of Nations," yet one can argue that in the case of the League, the father's role was the easiest. To quote Philip Noel Baker, it was Cecil the apostle who "brought the paper institution into life."[49] Cecil not only aided Wilson in creating the Covenant, but he also shielded the League from hostile forces. Many of the League's successes can be directy credited to this man's dogged devotion. He consolidated the limited gains of the revolution in international affairs, which the Covenant embodied, and continually reminded world politicians of the principles for which the League stood. In doing so, he proved a gallant fighter for peace and orderly process in some of the most violent years in human history. He accepted the position that the maintenance of peace might ultimately involve the use of the sword and was ready to act accordingly, but he sincerely believed there were other means, if honestly and actively pursued, that would render the need for arms remote. Indeed, Cecil's motto was the same as the quote he gave to the First Assembly in 1920: "Be just and fear not."[50]

Notes

1. *The Times* (London), December 20, 1920.
2. Gilbert Murray, *From the League to the U.N.* (New York: Oxford University Press, 1948), p. 71.
3. Charles F. Mullett, *Biography as History* (New York: Macmillan, 1963), p. 31.
4. W. N. Medlicott, *Contemporary England, 1914-1964* (London: Longmans, 1967), pp. 108-109. See also, Medlicott, *British Foreign Policy Since Versailles, 1919-1963* (London: Methuen and Co., Ltd., 1968), pp. 78-79.
5. F. S. Northedge, *The Troubled Giant* (London: G. Bell and Sons, 1966), p. 629.
6. Viscount Cecil of Chelwood (Lord Robert Cecil), *A Great Experiment* (London: Jonathan Cape, 1941), p. 159.
7. Viscount Cecil of Chelwood, *All the Way* (London: Hodder and Stoughton, 1949), pp. 13-14, 40, 241-242. See also Lady Gwendolyn Cecil, *Life of Robert, Marquis of Salisbury* (4 Vols., London: Hodder and Stoughton, 1921-1932); A. L. Kennedy, *Salisbury, 1830-1903: Portrait of a Statesman* (London: John Murray, 1953); Barbara Tuchman, *The Proud Tower: A Portrait of the World Before the War, 1890-1914* (New York: Macmillan, 1966), pp. 5-13.
8. Cecil, *All the Way*, p. 142. For a full account of the first two phases, see chapters II and III of *All the Way*; for Cecil's work with the League, see *A Great Experiment*.
9. A. J. P. Taylor, *The Troublemakers: Dissent over Foreign Policy, 1792-1939* (London: Hamish Hamilton, 1957), p. 187.
10. Jere Langdon Jackson, "Apostle of the League: Lord Robert Cecil and the Fight for the League of Nations, 1916-1924," (Unpublished Ph.D. dissertation, University of North Carolina, 1974); available on microfilm, University Microfilms, Ann Arbor, Michigan.
11. Burton J. Hendrick, *The Life and Letters of Walter Hines Page* (3 Vols., Garden City, New York: Doubleday, Page, and Company, 1922-1925), II, 209.
12. Edward Mandell House and Charles Seymour, *What Really Happened at Paris: The Story of the Peace Conference, 1918-1919* (New York: Charles Scribner's Sons, 1921), pp. 303-304.
13. Sir Oswald Mosley, *My Life* (London: Thomas Nelson, 1968), p. 148.
14. Lord Robert Cecil to Lord Salisbury (4th Marquis), May 18, 1921, Viscount Cecil of Chelwood Papers, British Museum. (Hereinafter cited as Cecil Papers, British Museum).

15. Robert Cecil to Ramsay MacDonald, June 23, 1924, Cecil Papers, British Museum.
16. On February 27, 1920, *The Times* (London), editorialized that Lloyd George in debate in the Commons recognized Cecil "not for the first time as his most formidable opponent." For one of the most cogent of Cecil's attacks on the Prime Minister's methods, see Great Britain, *House of Commons Debates*, 5th Series, Vol. 121 (November 17, 1919), col. 689. See also, *The Times*, (London), August 8, 1919, reporting a speech given by Cecil at The Center Party dinner club. For Cecil's full political program, see his *New Outlook* (London: Allen and Unwin, 1919). For comment on Cecil after he crossed the Aisle, see "Lord Robert Cecil's Future," reprinted from the *Manchester Guardian* in *Review of Reviews*, Vol. 63 (March, 1921), p. 314.
17. Cecil, *All the Way*, pp. 247-248. See also, Robert Cecil to Lord Salisbury, May 18, 1921; May 21, 1921, Cecil Papers, British Museum. William Ormsby-Gore warned Cecil that the ultra-Unionists would not join him: "They wouldn't look at you for your point of view is not reactionary." William Ormsby-Gore to Robert Cecil, no date (circa late January, 1921), Cecil Papers, British Museum.
18. For critical discussions of Lloyd George's methods, see: Harold Nicolson, *Curzon: Last Phase, 1919-1925* (Boston: Houghton Mifflin, 1934), pp. 54-55; Gordon A. Craig, "The British Foreign Office from Grey to Austen Chamberlain," *The Diplomats*, eds. G. A. Craig and Felix Gilbert (Princeton: Princeton University Press, 1953); Jere Langdon Jackson, "The Conference of Spa 1920: A Study in Postwar Conference Diplomacy," (Unpublished M. A. Thesis, George Washington University, 1965).
19. Mosley, *My Life*, pp. 136-140.
20. "Lord Robert Cecil's Future," reprinted from the *Manchester Guardian* in *Review of Reviews*, Vol. 63 (March, 1921), p. 314.
21. D. C. Watt, *Personalities and Politics: Studies in the Formulation of British Foreign Policy in the Twentieth Century* (Notre Dame: University Press, 1965), p. 35.
22. Jackson, "Cecil and the League of Nations," pp. 74-85, 137-142.
23. Nicolson, *Curzon*, pp. 37-39, 41-44.
24. *Ibid.*
25. *"The Draft Treaty of Mutual Assistance," Journal of the British Institute of International Affairs*, Vol. 3 No. 4 (March, 1924), pp. 60-68.
26. *The Times* (London), November 12 and 19, 1919; *House of Commons Debates*, 5th Series, Vol. 121 (November 17, 1919), Col. 689; *Ibid.*, Vol. 123 (December 18, 1919), Col. 734.
27. League of Nations, *Second Assembly*, 27th Plenary Session (October 1,

1921), pp. 646-647. For the interesting discussions on disarmament during the Second Assembly, see the Minutes of the Third Committee, pp. 329-339; for the report of the Third Committee written by Lord Robert Cecil, see Annex A, pp. 649-657.

28. Robert Cecil to Leon Bourgeois, February 17, 1922, Typescript Initialed Copy, Cecil Papers, British Museum.
29. League of Nations, *Records of the Third Assembly*, Minutes of the Third Committee, Annex 2, "Report of the Temporary Mixed Commission for the Reduction of Armaments," pp. 57-137. For a summary of the proposals he laid before the Third Committee, see Annex 3, "Draft Resolutions Submitted by Lord Robert Cecil to the Third Committee of the Assembly," pp. 138-139.
30. League of Nations, *Records of the Third Assembly*, Minutes of the Third Committee, Third Meeting, (September 12, 1922), pp. 16-17. For the initial reactions of the British to Cecil's proposals, see "Memorandum by Sir Cecil Hurst," July 26, 1922, Public Records Office, Foreign Office Papers FO 371/8331, with attached minutes by George Villiers and Sir William Terrell. For the Foreign Office response after the Third Assembly, see the Minute by Sir Eyre Crowe, December 18, 1922, FO 371/8319.
31. For a good discussion of the search for a security pact between Britain and France, see Chapter IX, Northedge, *The Troubled Giant*, pp. 223-247; also J. Paul Selsam, *The Attempts to Form an Anglo-French Alliance, 1919-1924* (Philadelphia: University of Pennsylvania Press, 1936), pp. 18 *et seq.*
32. Frank Walters, *A History of the League of Nations* (London: Oxford University Press, 1961), p. 225. For discussions of the Draft Treaty of Mutual Assistance, see, Cecil, *A Great Experiment*, pp. 138-141, 151-153; Kenneth Miller, *Socialism and Foreign Policy* (The Hague: Nijhoff, 1967), pp. 122-123; J. W. Wheeler-Bennett, *The Reduction of Armaments* (London: Allen and Unwin, 1925), pp. 77-89; Walters, *League of Nations*, pp. 215-228. James T. Shotwell and Marina Salvin, *Lessons on Security and Disarmament From the History of the League of Nations* (New York: Carnegie Endowment for Peace, 1949), pp. 16-23.
33. Andrew Martin, *Collective Security* (Paris: UNESCO, 1952), pp. 131-132.
34. J. M. Headlam-Morley to Eyre Crowe, Typescript Copy, July 8, 1923, Crowe's Private Collection, Foreign Office Papers, FO 800/243.
35. Lord Curzon to Robert Cecil, Confidential, July 10, 1923, Cecil Papers, British Museum. See also, Walters, *League of Nations*, pp. 242-243.

36. "Memorandum by Lord Robert Cecil on Reparations Policy," August 4, 1923, Cabinet Paper CP 376 (1923), Public Records Office, CAB 24/161.
37. Walters, *League of Nations*, p. 224.
38. For a recent account, see James Barros, *The Corfu Incident of 1923*: Mussolini and the League of Nations (Princeton, N.J.: Princeton University Press, 1965), pp. 215-217, 301. Many of Barros' conclusions are based upon too enthusiastic an acceptance of Harold Nicolson's biography of Curzon and the latter's view of himself contained in the Curzon Papers.
39. Barros, *The Corfu Incident*, p. 249. For the clearest summary of the incident and the British case at the time see, "Memorandum by Harold Nicolson," September 29, 1923, Public Records Office, FO 371/8621.
40. "Memorandum by Harold Nicolson," September 29, 1923, FO 371/8621; see also, Foreign Office Minutes, October 7-10, 1923, FO 371/8621.
41. Alan Cassels, *Mussolini's Early Diplomacy* (Princeton: Princeton University Press, 1970), pp. 118-120, 132, 217, 229-230.
42. Nicolson, *Curzon: Last Phase*, pp. 371-372.
43. "The Draft Treaty of Mutual Assistance," *Journal of the British Institute of International Affairs*, Vol. 3, No. 4 (March, 1924), pp. 60-68. See also, Joe Allen Thompson, "British Conservatives and Collective Security, 1918-1929," (Unpublished Ph.D. dissertation, Stanford University, 1966), pp. 56-62.
44. See Henry R. Winkler, "The Emergence of a Labor Foreign Policy in Great Britain, 1918-1929," *Journal of Modern History*, Vol. 28 (September, 1956), pp. 247 *et seq.* Winkler attributes the shift in Labour's attitude toward the League to Henderson, Clynes, and Noel-Baker, but fails to see that all three of these men were following in Cecil's wake.
45. J. Ramsay MacDonald, *The Foreign Policy of the Labour Party* (London: Palmer, 1923), pp. 20-21.
46. Norman Angell, *After All* (New York: Farrar, Straus, and Young, 1951), pp. 239-244.
47. Cmd. 2200, *Correspondence Between His Majesty's Government and the League of Nations Respecting the Proposed Treaty of Mutual Assistance*, Vol. XXVII (Misc. No. 4, 1924); for the drafting process of this note, see the documents in Foreign Office Papers FO 371/10568 during April and May of 1924. MacDonald's draft was primarily the work of Maurice Hankey and Eyre Crowe. For the additions forced on him by his own Cabinet, see Conclusions of the 35th Meeting of the Cabinet, May 30, 1924, CAB 23/48.

48. Taylor, *The Troublemakers*, p. 144.
49. Viscount Cecil, *All the Way*, p. 239.
50. League of Nations, *First Assembly*, 5th Plenary Session, November 17, 1920, pp. 93-99. The quote, "Be just and fear not," was taken from Shakespeare, *Henry VIII*, (III, ii, 443). Lord Robert's father had given this motto to the House of Lords in one of his greatest speeches; see A. L. Kennedy, *Salisbury*, p. 201.

9

The Cardinal's Sin

by
Maurice Williams
*Notre Dame University of Nelson,
British Columbia, Canada*

The German absorption of Austria on March 12, 1938, placed Theodor Innitzer, Austria's Roman Catholic Cardinal, in a precarious position. For centuries his Church had enjoyed the protection of a benevolent secular government. Now, with the National Socialist *Anschluss*, Innitzer recognized that this special relationship had ended. Additionally, he realized that his Church might suffer from its intimate association with the fallen Schuschnigg government. As a pillar of that defunct Austrian regime, the Church would probably come under attack. As Innitzer saw it, only if he could obtain a *modus vivendi*, an understanding with the Nazis, would he be able to safeguard clerical interests.

Naively Innitzer believed in those early days after *Anschluss* that he could reach a favorable accord with Adolf Hitler and the National Socialist hierarchy. Only slowly would he learn that neither bargaining nor trusting was possible with the Nazis. Yet before he learned this lesson, Innitzer would show a pronounced narrow-mindedness and selfishness, a willingness to ignore basic human rights and dignity for the sake of preserving the Church. In his negotiations with the Nazis, the Cardinal would seek merely a special status for Roman Catholicism; he would make no attempt to defend individual or civil rights. Innitzer would indicate by his action that he agreed with the Italian Prelate, Nuncio Sibilia: as long as the Nazis guaranteed clerical control of marriage and education, the Church could support the fascist movement.[1]

Innitzer began his quest for an understanding easily enough. On March 13, the Cardinal published a statement in the Catholic newspaper, the *Reichspost*, urging all persons in the Vienna diocese to offer prayers for the bloodless course of the recent revolution; further, he instructed them to pray for a happy Austrian future.[2] Implying acceptance of German control, his statement actually reflected more than a mere outward toleration of the *Anschluss*. Innitzer, after all, came from the Sudetenland, where the sense of being "German" had been an emotional issue since the late nineteenth century. In March, 1933, when he became a Cardinal, he outlined his feelings: "I am a true son of my church just as I am a true son of my German *Volk*."[3] Privately, Innitzer believed a Christian German nation, a country in which Austria joined Germany, would be the ideal state for Central Europe. As a German nationalist, therefore, he had no difficulty reconciling the *Anschluss*. What concerned him was the status of the Church, especially since he was well aware of the *Kulturkampf* in National Socialist Germany. Consequently, his statement in the *Reichspost* was the first step toward appeasing the Nazis, a first step toward obtaining the necessary *modus vivendi*.[4]

Within three days of the *Anschluss* the Cardinal shared his sentiments directly with Adolf Hitler. On March 15, at a meeting arranged by Franz von Papen, the German ambassador in Vienna, they discussed the place of Austrian Catholics in the new order. Innitzer declared that a German mentality had always been present in Austria; citizens had opposed the *Anschluss* only because of the revolutionary Nazi methods. Now that union had occurred, he claimed, Austrian Catholics would become the most faithful sons of the great Reich, provided, of course, that the Church and schools continued to enjoy the freedoms verified in the 1934 Austria-Rome Concordat. Hitler, obviously overjoyed at the expression of loyalty, shook Innitzer's hand warmly but typically promised everything. He assured the Cardinal that cooperation would guarantee that the Church had nothing to fear.[5] Innitzer, visibly pleased, commented later: "It appears that you can talk with this man."[6]

The Viennese Cardinal, however, quickly found his expectation short-lived. While he anticipated radio and press coverage of the meeting and its results, to his astonishment only the *Reichspost* carried an account. Even that paper's version was one-sided, reporting that the Cardinal had expressed pleasure at the Austro-German union and that he stood ready to work energetically for reconstruction of the country. The article failed to mention Hitler's promises.[7]

Hardly had Innitzer absorbed this example of the new "cooperation" when he was confronted by an ironic demand from Josef Buerckel, the recently appointed Nazi plenipotentiary in Austria. What position, Buerckel asked, would the Catholic bishops take concerning the forthcoming April 10 plebescite, the ex post facto acceptance or rejection of the *Anschluss*?[8] Innitzer realized that his response would have to satisfy the Nazis completely, yet at the same time protect the Church. Unfortunately for the Cardinal and his fellow bishops, an independent reply was doomed when the Nazis approached Innitzer with the wording of a response, which the Nazis termed a loyalty declaration. Innitzer explained to his colleagues what Josef Himmelreich, Buerckel's representative, told him: "If it [the loyalty declaration] is down in writing then the peace between church and state is complete."[9] After discussing the proposal at a meeting on March 18, Austria's bishops dutifully signed the proposed document; now perhaps, Innitzer hoped, they had an effective arrangement.

The declaration, one of the most important propaganda tools the Germans used in their April plebescite campaign, began by asserting that the bishops made the statement voluntarily. Citing the outstanding Nazi achievements in reconstructing the German Reich, it noted in particular the halting of the dangerous spread of Bolshevism. But most importantly, the bishops agreed to do their "national duty" on April 10; they would declare themselves Germans of the Reich, and they would expect the same from other faithful Christians.[10]

At first Innitzer agreed to the declaration without reservation. Within several hours, however, he realized that the statement, hastily accepted, might be misunderstood by his fellow Austrians. He added, therefore, a clarifying preamble. Joined by his fellow archbishop, Sigismund Waitz of Salzburg, he specified that the motto, "Render unto God the things which are God's, and unto

Caesar the things which are Caesar's," applied to the bishops' recent statement.[11]

But the Cardinal was not finished. In forwarding the Bishop's Declaration and Preamble to Buerckel, Innitzer added a covering letter. After dictating the correspondence, the Cardinal asked Himmelreich, who had arrived to receive the material, how to close the letter. Himmelreich replied that customarily the German bishops signed "Heil Hitler." Despite the fact that many of his countrymen and friends languished in prison because of this same Hitler, Innitzer complied.[12]

Again, the National Socialists stunned the Cardinal. They immediately printed one million copies of the Bishops' Declaration along with facsimilies of Innitzer's "Heil Hitler" letter and circulated these propaganda leaflets in Austria and Germany. Astounded, Innitzer had not envisioned such a distorted usage of the proclamation. Instead, he had believed sincerely that the Bishops had fulfilled their half of a bargain: in return for the private loyalty declaration, the National Socialist regime would guarantee the Church's rights of independence, its freedoms in pastoral care, and especially its control of schools and the education of youth. Himmelreich, in fact, had conveyed these very assurances, but as the Cardinal soon realized, he had only vague promises.[13]

Beyond the dismay which Innitzer felt, his involvement with the loyalty declaration placed him in an awkward position; in fact, the entire matter brought him little save trouble and condemnation. To begin, the Vatican severely censured him and his colleagues for their action. The Vatican Radio exclaimed that "these pastors no longer recognize the wolf in sheep's clothing as is their duty."[14] Then, Pope Pius XI summoned Innitzer to Rome for an accounting; as a result of their lengthy audience, the Cardinal issued yet another Proclamation clarifying his position. The Austrian primate stated he did not approve of documents incompatible with the laws of God or with the liberty and rights of the Catholic Church. Further, he added, the National Socialists should not exploit clerical statements for propaganda purposes.[15] But the damage was done. Innitzer could not turn back the clock to March 17. Actually, his Roman retraction, even though not reported in the National Socialist press, brought sharp rebukes from the Nazis. Buerckel declared that the favorable feeling between Church and state was shattered; on April 9 Hitler personally expressed disapproval. "I wanted to make a binding declaration with reference to the Catholic Church in Austria," he claimed. "After your declaration in Rome, however, I must distance myself from it."[16] The Austrian primate, therefore, gained nothing from either the Declaration or its retraction; the Nazis, on the other hand, had both their propaganda and an "excuse" not to honor their vague pledges.

Amazingly, Innitzer addressed yet another letter to Buerckel in which he concluded with "Heil Hitler" for a second time. An abridgement of this letter — with its "Heil Hitler" intact — was published in all the leading German papers just in time to aid the plebescite campaign, thereby again compromising the Austrian Cardinal.[17]

Despite the problems and blunders, Innitzer somehow hoped he could still reach an understanding with the Nazis since he felt a sense of increasing urgency. In Styria, the bishop had been jailed for twenty-four hours; clergy were imprisoned; Roman Catholic journalists were arrested. In upper Austria, churches, parsonages, and clerical institutions had been "searched for weapons." The dioceses of Salzburg, Linz, St. Poelten, Gurk, and Seckau reported similar threats.[18] By early May Innitzer faced even more severe measures. The Nazis sent special commissioners to all monasteries and abbeys to make inventories of valuables and possessions; based on these reports some two hundred cloisters, convents, and clerical houses were eventually closed and their goods confiscated. The Nazis also seized Roman Catholic presses and publishing houses, including eleven dailies, which were either closed or placed under Nazi direction. Libraries and reading rooms suffered a similar fate; in Vienna, 700,000 volumes from clerical borrowing houses were appropriated or destroyed.[19]

Yet Innitzer's most serious problem concerned the 1934 Concordat between Austria and Rome. Were the rights and prerogatives outlined for the Austrian Church still valid? Or more to Innitzer's point, did the agreement itself remain in force? If it was not valid, Innitzer wondered had the German Concordat of 1933 superceded it?

Hitler settled the questions for the Cardinal on July 12, 1938. He ruled that the 1934 Concordat had expired when Austria joined the Reich; he further stated that since Austria had not been a part of Germany when Berlin and Rome signed their 1933 agreement, the German treaty did not automatically extend to Austria. Consequently, Austria had no Concordat of any kind "for the time."[20] Innitzer was horrified; the prospects of negotiating a *modus vivendi* had suffered another crippling blow. Hitler's pronouncement meant the Cardinal faced grave problems; indeed, he confronted a full fledged *Kulturkampf*.

With the Austrians religiously unprotected, the Nazis attacked the most important areas of clerical strength and privilege — education, youth, and marriage. They struck systematically. On July 19 the National Socialist state withdrew recognition and rights from the nearly 1000 private Catholic schools. By September most of these schools had been secularized or closed completely.[21] During the late summer the government also reduced the traditional religious instruction in the public schools as well as in the professional, trade, and training schools. By September 17 the government ruled it was no longer compulsory for students to attend religious classes; a further decree stipulated that pupils over fourteen years of age, not their parents, could decide for themselves whether or not they would participate.[22] Meanwhile, the Nazis dissolved church youth groups, disbanded religious clubs, and confiscated property belonging to the disappearing organizations. Young people, the Nazis made it clear, could join only three associations — the Hitler Youth, the German Young People, and the Band of German Maidens. Each group, of course, was sponsored by the National Socialists.[23] The Nazis further attacked the clerical monopoly of marriage and divorce. A decree of July 12 ordered state marriages after August 1; church ceremonies were completely optional.[24]

In spite of this atmosphere, Innitzer still tried to negotiate with the National Socialist hierarchy; his attempts faltered on every conceivable obstacle. Typically, a meeting scheduled for September 8 with Buerckel broke down when the Cardinal discovered just before the session that the Nazis had dissolved two more important monastic orders. He had little choice but to cancel the meeting.[25] An attempt to draw Hitler into the fray also experienced a similar failure. On September 28 Innitzer and his colleagues sent the *Fuehrer* a personal letter outlining the Austrian church situation since *Anschluss*. They noted that all compromise attempts with Buerckel had failed; now only he, Hitler, could successfully resolve the difficulties. Nothing came of the letter, however, as the Fuehrer did not even decide against replying until February, 1939.[26]

Innitzer, thus compromised, humiliated, and dishonored, had only one option remaining if he was to protect the Church; he must rally Roman Catholics and present a strong front against the Nazi aggressors. Consequently, after weeks of harrassment and degradation, Innitzer asserted the strong leadership that he had failed to express at the time of *Anschluss*. He realized at last what National Socialism meant to his Church. In August he led fellow bishops in taking a firm position against the mandatory civil marriage; a pastoral letter of August 19 obliged Roman Catholics to subscribe to a church wedding. He also criticized the Nazis for withdrawing recognition of Catholic schools.[27] Later, in early September, Innitzer utilized the pulpit to attack National Socialism; he closed one sermon by declaring:

> They have already taken our schools, given us beautiful promises, and in the end given us nothing. The Bishop of Vienna is greatly disillusioned. But do not lose courage; stay true to the faith.[28]

On September 20, Innitzer strengthened his control over the clergy by ordering severe ecclesiastical penalties for any priest who joined the Nazi association of clerics—the Union for Religious Peace.[29] Two days later he entreated Roman Catholic parents to keep their children in religious classes at school; at the same time they should stress religious education at home.[30]

This budding sense of independence and display of leadership, however, came to an abrupt halt in the second week of October. Events of October 8 and October 13 frightened Innitzer sufficiently that he never again spoke out against National Socialism. He became, in effect, the silent Cardinal of Austria.

The October 8 episode began with the young people of the Vienna diocese. Since the *Anschluss* of the previous March the Church had made special efforts to strengthen its ties with teenagers. When the Nazis began dissolving all but the purely religious clubs, the Church encouraged groups of young people to attend worship services together. Part of that practice was a mass at St. Stephens Cathedral marking the beginning of the school year. While the cathedral staff expected some 2500 young people for the service on October 7, 7000 teenagers filled the church.[31] Innitzer, who led the worship, was not an exceptional preacher, but his words carried added force that evening as he exhorted:

> You have lost nearly everything in the past month. You have lost your Catholic clubs and your Christian unions; but in spite of the fact that you have been deprived of all that you will gather in new Catholic union with your priests . . . We must give first to the Lord God what belongs to him, and then we will fulfill also the other duties; He will then give us strength, the inner peace, the joy. The words 'Strength through Joy' have a deep meaning.[32]

When the service ended church officials encouraged the congregation to return home quietly and quickly, especially since members of the Hitler Youth reportedly waited to take the names of worshippers. Instead, however, the young people joined a spontaneous demonstration before the Archbishop's palace. Voices cried, "We greet our Bishop; we greet our Bishop." "We want to see our Bishop; we want to see our Bishop." After Innitzer had made a brief appearance the cries grew louder, "We thank our Bishop; God bless our Bishop." Soon the words of an old Tyrolian hymn could be heard: "Yes, we swear today anew, Jesus Christ to you eternally true." Only after the hymn had been repeated several times did the young people slowly disperse.[33]

The National Socialists responded quickly to this display of teenage loyalty. The next evening, October 8, some 100 youths attacked the archbishop's palace. They broke over 1000 windows, battered down the front gate, destroyed furniture, slashed valuable paintings, desecrated images of the saints and crucifixes, plundered the cardinal's clothes closet, stole his religious jewelry, and threatened two clerical associates with physical harm (six youths picked up one priest shouting, "We'll throw the dog out the window.") Innitzer escaped injury only by hiding in the library vault. Meanwhile others attacked the rectory of the Cathedral, this time actually throwing one curate from a second story window. Exactly forty minutes after the demonstration began, the chief of the Vienna police force, who had been sitting across the courtyard sipping coffee, ordered the rioters dispersed. Naturally the police failed to apprehend the guilty. Yet the Cardinal and his household received orders not to leave the building until the investigation had finished. Although the police did not use the term "house arrest," Innitzer understood their intent.[34]

Scarcely had a week passed before the Nazis reinforced their displeasure with the Cardinal; the National Socialists wanted to insure that the Archbishop understood that "silent men live to enjoy old age." On Thursday evening, October 13, the leader of the Viennese Nazi party, Odilio Globocnik, "invited" demonstrators against the Church to gather on Helden Plaza. The party faithful assembled, toting their placards: "Down with the clerics." "Innitzer to Dachau." "Without Jews, without Rome, we will build Germany's *Dom*."[35] Globocnik spoke briefly, then introduced Josef Buerckel, who talked of settling accounts with the Church; Buerckel revealed that clerical deceitfulness (i.e., the spontaneous youth demonstration of October 7) had nullified any agreements reached with the Church. Thus the Nazi leadership publicly blessed the *Kulturkampf*.[36]

The finale for that evening saw the crowd burn Innitzer in effigy, followed by a march to the Archbishop's Palace. "Down with Innitzer," they cried. "We don't need priests." "Send the dog Innitzer to the gallows." Occasionally someone fired a pistol into the air, but for the most part the demonstration remained under control.[37]

The message was clear. First the October 8 demonstration, and then the October 13 rally convinced the Cardinal of his fate if he defied the Nazis or challenged their leadership. He realized that survival, not a *modus vivendi*, was the main objective of the Austrian Church. He therefore determined that silence was his safest option, never again speaking against National Socialism nor leading his Church against the State. He had attempted to negotiate with "honorable men," as he told Josef Himmelreich after the war, but had been "disgracefully deceived."[38] So while other clerics suffered (one of every eight Austrian priests was arrested, imprisoned, interned, or executed during the next seven years), Innitzer kept his silence, dying peacefully in 1955, still the Catholic Cardinal of Austria. He had proven once again that the institutional Church could survive nearly anything—humiliation, sacrifice, even a silent, irresolute leader.

Notes

1. Friedrich Heer, *God's First Love; Christians and Jews Over Two Thousand Years*, trans. by Geoffrey Skelton (London: Weidenfeld & Nicolson, 1970), pp. 272-273.
2. "Austrian Primate's Advice," *Manchester Guardian*, March 14, 1938, Press Archive, Wiener Library, London.
3. Viktor Reimann, *Innitzer, Kardinal zwischen Hitler und Rom* (Vienna: Verlag Fritz Molden, 1967), p. 58 (Hereafter cited as Reimann, *Innitzer*).
4. "Der Bericht des Dr. [Josef] Himmelreich," n.d., n.pl., in Hans Jablonka, *Weitz, Bishof unter Kaiser und Hitler* (Vienna: Dom-Verlag, 1971), p. 96. (Hereafter cited as "Bericht des Himmelreich." Main entry hereafter cited as Jablonka, *Weitz*.) U.S., National Archives, Office of Strategic Services, *The Roman Catholic Church In Austrian Political Life*, Washington, January 11, 1945, Research and Analysis Report 2338.
5. "Treatise by Franz von Papen on Austria," May 3, 1945, Document Number PS 3300, *Nazi Conspiracy And Aggression* (10 vols.; Washington: Government Printing Office, 1946-1948), A, 501; Franz von Papen, *Der Wahrheit eine Gasse* (Innsbruck: Paul List Verlag, 1952), pp. 491-492; Jakob Fried, *Nationalsozialismus und katholische Kirche in Oesterreich* (Vienna: Wiener Dom-Verlag, 1947), p. 23. (Hereafter cited as Fried, *Nationalsozialismus und Kirche*.)
6. "Oesterreichs Christenzwischen 1938 und 1945," *St. Poeltner Kirchenzeitung,* November 26, 1961, p. 12; Karl Rudolf, *Aufbau im Widerstand; Ein Seelsorgebericht aus Oesterreich, 1938-1945* (Salzburg: Otto Mueller Verlag, 1947), p. 18.
7. Erika Weinzierl-Fischer. "Oesterreichs Katholiken und der Nationalsozialismus," *Wort und Wahrheit*, XVIII (August/September, 1963), 509.
8. Buerckel had the responsibility of preparing the country for the April 10 plebiscite and after the fact Austrian acceptance or rejection of the *Anschluss*. Fried, *Nationalsozialismus und Kirche*, p. 24.
9. Josef Himmelreich Brief, May 1, 1955, in Reimann, *Innitzer*, p. 111. See also "Bericht des Himmelreich," pp. 91-92; Karl Barth Memorandum, Obermohr, Austria, February 21, 1955, in Jablonka, *Weitz*, pp. 84-88.
10. "Feierliche Erklaerung," Vienna, March 21, 1938, *Ursachen und*

Folgen; Vom Deutschen Zusammenbruch 1918 und 1945 bis zu Staatlichen Neuordnung Deutschlands in der Gegenwart, Vol. XI: *Das Dritte Reich* (Berlin: Dokumenten-Verlag Dr. Herbert Wendler & Co., 1966), pp. 677-678. (Main entry hereafter cited as *Ursachen und Folgen; Das Dritte Reich*.)

11. Letter from Theodor Innitzer and Sigismund Waitz to Josef Buerckel, Vienna, March 21, 1938, *Ursachen und Folgen; Das Dritte Reich*, pp. 677-678.
12. *Ibid.*; "Bericht des Himmerlreich," p. 95.
13. Great Britain, Public Record Office, Ogilvie-Forbes to Halifax, Annual Report for Germany, 1938, Berlin, January 27, 1939, C1360/1360/18; "Bericht des Himmelreich," pp. 97-98.
14. Vatican Radio, April 1, 1938, Arnold J. Toynbee, *Survey of International Relations, 1938* (3 vols.; London: Oxford University Press, 1941), I, 248. See also The German Ambassador to the Holy See (Bergen) to the German Foreign Ministry, Rome, April 1, 1938, *Documents on German Foreign Policy, 1918-45*, Series D, 1937-45, Vol. I: *From Neurath to Ribbentrop (September 1937-September 1938)* (Washington: Government Printing Office, 1949), p. 1028.
15. "Erklaerung Kardinal Innitzers in Rom zur Erklaerung der oesterreichischen Bishoefen vom 18. Maerz," Rome, April 6, 1938, Otto Frass, ed., *Quellenbuch zur Oesterreichischen Geschichte* (4 vols.; Vienna: Birken-Verlag, 1967), IV, p. 250.
16. "Bericht des Himmelreich," p. 100; Fried, Nationalsozialismus und Kirche, p. 28.
17. Letter from Theodor Innitzer to Josef Buerckel, Vienna, March 31, 1938, *Ursachen und Folgen; Das Dritte Reich*, pp. 678-679.
18. "Die Kirchenverfolgung in der Steiermark," n.pl., n.d., unpublished material compiled for *Rot-Weiss-Rot*, folder entitled "Kirches," Dokumentationsarchiv des oesterreichischen Widerstandes, Vienna, Austria. (Dokumentationsarchiv des oesterreichischen Widerstandes hereafter cited as DOW.) "Congregation des Lazaristen in Graz, Bedrangnisse und Verluste durch die nationalsozialistische Regierung," Graz, April 28, 1946, unpublished material compiled for *Rot-Weiss-Rot*, folder entitled "Kirches," DOW; "Bericht des Pfarramtes Argen i. M., Abschrift," April 21, 1946, unpublished material compiled for *Rot-Weiss-Rot*, folder entitled "Oberoesterreich," *DOW*; "Bericht ueber die Jahre 1938 bis 1945," Pfarramt Ulrichsberg, April 20, 1946, unpublished material compiled for *Rot-Weiss-Rot*, DOW.
19. Statement by Bishop Paulus Rusch, Innsbruck, June 27, 1945, Document 3278-PS, *Trial of the Major War Criminals Before The*

International Military Tribunal (42 vols.; Nuremberg, Germany, 1947-1949), XXXII, 126-127; Toynbee, *Survey of International Relations, 1938*, I, 250-251; Jakob Fried, "Mein Leben in der Nazizeit" (unpublished manuscript, Vienna, 1947), Document Number 4748, DOW.

20. Der Reichsminister und Chef der Reichskanzlei (Lammers) an die Herrn Reichsministern, Berlin, July 12, 1938, Document Number 4987, DOW.
21. U.S., National Archives, "Bericht ueber die kirchliche Lage in der Erzdioezese Salzburg seit Maerz 1938," by the Prince Archbishop of Salzburg, September 24, 1945, Shuster Mission, Interrogation Reports, Record Group 165; *Mitteilungen zur Weltanschaulichen Lage; Der Beauftragte des Fuehrers fuer die Gesamte Geistige und Weltanschauliche Erziehung des NSDAP*, Sonderausgabe, May, 1939, pp. 3/4-4/5. (Hereafter cited as *Mitteilungen zur Weltanschaulichen Lage*.)
22. "Schulwesen," *Wiener Dioezesanblatt*, July 18, 1938; "Teilnahme der Schuler an Religionsunterricht und an religioesen Uebunger," *St. Poeltener Dioezensanblatt,* October 13, 1938, pp. 142-143; *Mitteilungen zur Weltanschaulichen Lage*, pp. 6/7.
23. Great Britain, Public Record Office, Consul-General to Berlin Embassy, June Report, July 1, 1938, C6828/62/18; Geheime Staatspolizei in Wien an die Geheime Staatspolizei, Berlin, July 3, 1938, Film #100, DOW.
24. "Einfuehrung des obligatorische Zivilehe in Lande Oesterreich," *Wiener Dioezesanblatt*, July 18, 1938, p. 65.
25. "Bericht des Himmelreich," pp. 117-118; Letter from Theodor Innitzer to Josef Buerckel, Vienna, September 7, 1938, Frass, *Quellenbuch zur Oesterreichischen Geschichte*, IV, 247.
26. Staff Analysis Report, Nurnberg, Summarization of a request to Josef Buerckel from Adolf Hitler to answer the Bishop's charges, February 17, 1939, Document Number NG-4970, Insitut fuer Zeitgeschichte, Munich, Germany.
27. "An die Katholischer Brautleute!" *Wiener Dioezesan-Blatt*, August, 1938, p. 87. See also Gestapo Tagesrapport, #5, Vienna, September 6, 1938, Microfilm Number T 84, R13, 40066-40067, National Archives, Washington, D.C.
28. Theodor Innitzer Sermon, September 17, 1938, in Reiman, *Innitzer*, p. 187.
29. "Verbot der 'Arbeitsgemeinschaft fuer den religiosen Freiden fuer Priesten," *St. Poeltener Dioezesanblatt*, October 13, 1938, p. 142; Gestapo Tagesrapport, #2, Vienna, October 3, 1938, Microfilm Number T84, R13, 39943, National Archives, Washington, D.C.

30. "Ein Wort an die Katholischen Eltern," *Wiener Dioesesanblatt*, September 30, 1938, p. 126.
31. Great Britain, Foreign Office, Political Intelligence Department, *Austria: Basic Handbook*, Part I: "Geographical, Political and Social" (London: Foreign Office, 1944), chap. V.; "Oesterreichs Christen zwischen 1938 und 1945," *St. Poeltner Kirchenzeitung*, February 25, 1962, p. 12.
32. Theodor Innitzer Sermon, October 7, 1938, in Toynbee, *Survey of International Relations, 1938*, I, 252.
33. Gestapo Tagesrapport, #7, Vienna, October 11, 12, 1938, Microfilm Number T84, R13, 39906-39907, National Archive, Washington, D.C.; Reiman, *Innitzer*, pp. 190, 290.
34. Gestapo Tagesrapport, Vienna, October 8, 10, 1938, Microfilm Number T84, R13, 39898-39899, National Archive, Washington, D.C.; "Aussagen des erzbishoeflichen Sekretaers Domkapitular Weinbacher betr. den Uberfall auf das Palais des Kardinals Innitzer in Wien am 8 Oktober 1938," *Ursachen und Folgen; Das Dritte Reich*, pp. 693-695.
35. *Neue Freie Presse*, October 13, 1938, Christine Klusacek, Herbert Steiner, and Kurt Stimmer, eds., *Dokumentation zur Oesterreichischen Zeitgeschichte* 1938-1945 (Vienna: Jugend und Volk, 1971), p. 12; October 13, 1938, *Keesings Archiv der Gegenwart* (Vienna: Elbemuehl Papierfabriken und graphische Industrie A.G., n.d.), p. 3762.
36. Gestapo Tagesrapport, #8, Vienna, October 13, 14, 1938, Microfilm Number T84, R13, 31896-31897; October 13, 1938, *Keesings Archiv Der Gegenwart*, p. 3762.
37. Gestapo Tagesrapport, #8, Vienna, October 13, 14, 1938; *Neue Freie Presse*, October 14, 1938, Klusacek, Steiner, and Stimmer, *Dokumentation zur Oesterreichischen Zeitgeschichte 1938-1945*, p. 99.
38. "Bericht des Himmelreich," p. 119.

10

The Conservative Reaction To The Peace Ballot

by
E. Deanne Malpass
Stephen F. Austin State University

On September 11, 1935, Sir Samuel Hoare, speaking on behalf of Great Britain at Geneva, startled the delegates and the world by suddenly becoming a staunch advocate of the League of Nations and collective security. Formerly lukewarm at best when the League faced a crisis, the British Conservative government appeared determined to stop Mussolini in his Ethiopian venture. If Hoare's words and gestures meant what they implied, British policy had undergone a striking change. What had induced this apparent about-face?

Between November, 1934, and June, 1935, a great unofficial polling of British public opinion had taken place. Lord Robert Cecil, an ardent League statesman, inspired the canvass to combat "Beaverbrook's isolationism" and "defeatism" regarding the League of Nations. Although he denied any intention of "embarrassing" the government, Cecil later expressed the hope that the ballot would move the administration into line with the national will. Popularly known as the Peace Ballot, the plan was adopted at a general council meeting of the League of Nations Union in the spring of 1934.[1] Under Union auspices the referendum quickly drew support from a number of political parties, churches, and service groups, whose members helped distribute, collect, tabulate and analyze the results. The public voted on five major policy questions:

1. Should Great Britian remain a member of the League of Nations?
2. Are you in favor of an all-around reduction of armaments by international agreement?

3. Are you in favor of an all-around abolition of national and military and naval aircraft by international agreement?
4. Should the manufacture and sale of armaments for private profits be prohibited by international agreement?
5. Do you consider that, if a nation insists on attacking another, the other nations should combine to compel it to stop by
   (a) Economic and non-military measures?
   (b) If necessary, military measures?[2]

At first, members from all three major parties responded warmly to the non-partisan referendum. Conservative support for the enterprise, however, proved distinctly less enthusiastic than that of Liberal and Labour party members, who viewed the Peace Ballot as an opportunity to force the National government to take a stand in favor of collective security. When the questions to be voted on were announced in June, 1934, Conservative coolness increased and "gravest objections" were expressed concerning the poll.[3]

By late July Conservative coolness had changed to outspoken opposition, which culminated in a vocal and vehement campaign aimed at discrediting the referendum and its backers. Col. George Herbert, speaking for the Conservative Party, opened the attack by advising local leaders not to co-operate in the canvass.

Expressing concern over the futility of such a survey, Herbert pointed out that although the first two questions on the ballot appeared straightforward, the last three contained serious pitfalls. In his opinion their "bald form" obscured their intrinsic complexity and such questions could not be answered with a simple "yes" or "no." The ballot, therefore, could be of no significance. To the degree that it might force the government to adopt inexpedient policies, it would be distinctly harmful, he argued.[4] Herbert hinted that the ballot probably was a political plot designed to disparage the government.

His insinuations were denied by Cecil and League supporters, of course, but Conservative opposition continued. Many party agents refused to give referendum workers access to their voting lists and hampered those efforts in every possible way. At the request of the party Conservative M. P.'s worked to combat the Peace Ballot in their own constituencies.[5]

As the collection of ballot papers began, leading Conservatives derided the poll, its purpose and its supporters. Sir Austin Chamberlain led the attack. Although a member of the League of Nations Union, he had joined at the request of Conservative leaders to keep an eye on Union activities. By July, totally out of sympathy with the ballot, he proclaimed his membership in the League of Nations Union a "shirt of Nessus," which he could no longer endure. He remained, nevertheless, a member of the Union's executive committee and lobbied throughout the summer for changes in the poll. When the Union tried to meet his objections by issuing a "green" sheet to clarify the ballot questions, Chamberlain angrily contended that the answers were weighted. Under the watchful eye of Conservatives the Union then drew up a new "blue" paper, but it also failed to win Chamberlain's approval. Finally a compromise "yellow" paper was prepared, and local branches were given the option of using the blue-green papers together or the yellow paper alone. The battle of the colored sheets satisfied no one and confused the public.[6]

By November Chamberlain's opposition was so great that many were convinced he would surely resign from the Union.[7] Instead Sir Austin, although retaining his membership, openly attacked the ballot in Parliament. Describing the canvass as a "fraudulent prospectus" foisted upon the public, Chamberlain impugned the integrity of Cecil and other ballot promoters. Though he subsequently denied any such intent, his speech nevertheless "disheartened" and "bewildered" many who supported the poll.[8]

Sir John Simon, Secretary of State for Foreign Affairs, agreed with Chamberlain's assessment of the ballot. Simon damned it as deliberately rigged to obtain favorable answers by "hook or crook." Although conceding that some of the questions might be "proper," he considered most of them oversimplifications. The Peace Ballot required uncommon answers from the common man, Simon charged, and he questioned the ability of the "uninstructed" citizen to arrive at sound conclusions. Both Chamberlain and Simon hinted that the ballot was little more than a political gambit, and other Conservatives echoed the charge.[9]

Among them, Duff Cooper labeled the ballot "Cecil's poisonous propaganda," while Philip Cunliffe-Lister, Secretary of State for the Colonies, and Sir Bolton Eyres-Monsell, First Lord of the Admiralty, bitterly characterized it as a "dishonest" machination of the Labour Party.[10] Never a friend of the League of Nations Union, Stanley Baldwin, the real leader of the Conservative Party, harshly condemned the ballot and its backers when he addressed the annual Conference of Scottish Unionist Associations in Glasgow. Baldwin, who had once refused a Union speaking engagement on the grounds that he would be forced to "steer between the Scylla of cursing them and the Charybdis of mush and poppycock," now declared the referendum was "unscrupulous" politics of the "lowest kind." He warned the League of Nations Union that such political activities could destroy "irrevocably" both its organization and its usefulness.[11]

Leopold Amery, one of the most vitriolic antagonists of the ballot, speaking at a Conservative Conference at Leeds, pictured the 500,000 referendum volunteers as an army of "sincere if muddleheaded pacifists and panic mongers" being led to disaster by "astute political gangsters." At a time when world conditions were forcing a normally pacifist National government to take defensive measures, he charged that this "insidious" campaign was an effort to sap the ministry's strength from within. If the guileless voted yes to the Peace Ballot, they would unwittingly endorse the Socialist Party and consequently work against the national interest.[12]

As befitted the Labour head of a "National" government, Prime Minister Ramsay MacDonald chose his words cautiously in commenting upon the Peace Ballot. He had always disliked the Union intensely because he felt the organization had scorned his support in the past. The speech he delivered at Southampton in mid-November, therefore, despite his usual vague, rambling style, was very clear. Picturing the canvass as a "strange agitation" promising attractive but "unsubstantial things," MacDonald tagged it a device to smear his government and indignantly repudiated the implication that his ministry was lacking in zeal for peace. In his opinion the questions on the ballot were designed to divide and weaken Britain, and nothing but mischief could result.[13]

The *Times*, of course, echoed the government's line and ridiculed the poll. Contending that the Peace Ballot had already gained far more attention than it merited, the editor extended sympathy to those who refused to support a "gratuitous" and "pointless" survey. Although some readers might remain sincerely puzzled by the canvass, he declared that the wisest recognized it as a "stunt" and had forwarded their ballots to "the most suitable destination," a trash can.[14]

Why did Conservatives denounce the Peace Ballot so vehemently? Was it really as dangerous as they portrayed it? Was it actually a threat to the peace or security of Britain?

Despite their charges of oversimplification, party politics, and pacifist nonsense, were there not more profound reasons for their opposition? From the Conservative viewpoint, the Peace Ballot could hardly have been timed worse. It raised questions on policy at a moment when the government, bent on rearmament and balance of power diplomacy, found such public soul-searching embarrassing. In the fall of 1934 nothing could have been less fortuitous than a national survey that would intensify support for the League, collective security, and disarmament.

Apparently it had been quite by chance that the government announced its campaign to expand the air force at the very moment when the people of Britain were asked to vote on the question of reducing armaments. To numerous League supporters, the government's program seemed needlessly expensive and represented a betrayal of the Disarmament Conference. The League of Nations Union, in a hastily drawn resolution, which alienated many Conservatives, pledged to resist the increase.[15] In Parliament Lord Cecil led the opposition to the government's air program, maintaining that international peace was, after all, the only real defense against air attack. In his opinion, increasing the air force was therefore unrealistic, and the government would thereby diminish or destroy the last hope for the Disarmament Conference. Even if, as some argued, the Disarmament Conference really was moribund, Cecil felt the government's announcement should have waited until its official close. By such unfortunate timing, the government appeared to have abandoned all hope or plans for armament reduction. Cecil's stand impressed many because he, though nominally a Conservative, placed his loyalty to the principle of collective security above party considerations. It was wormwood and gall for his fellow party members that he should be the leading advocate of the Peace Ballot.[16]

In addition, Conservatives deplored the Union's action in raising questions regarding the private sale of armaments. In the United States the recent Nye Committee investigations, which appeared to link munitions manufacturing and profiteering as a contributory cause of war, had aroused enormous interest in Great Britain. The public flooded the government with demands for a similar inquiry, and by November this pressure forced a reluctant administration to yield. Tories held the Peace Ballot responsible.[17]

For most Conservatives, however, the really disconcerting issue raised by the referendum concerned collective security. The imminence of war between Italy and Ethiopia made the question regarding the imposition of economic and military sanctions an especially delicate one for the British government.[18] At the same time, growing apprehensions over German resurgence, heightened by Hitler's withdrawal from the Disarmament Conference in 1933, added to the gravity of the international situation. In the eyes of government leaders, collective security appeared to be a chimera luring Britain to disaster.

Baldwin created a furor in the midst of the canvass when he publicly depicted collective security as "perfectly impracticable" if any major power remained outside the League. He would not, he avowed, ever vote to impose League sanctions unless he knew what the United States intended to do.[19] Although Baldwin's explicit statement aroused a storm of protest among League disciples, Prime Minister Ramsay MacDonald refused to repudiate his colleague's stand. Instead MacDonald also averred that collective security was technically unworkable without League "universality."[20]

Despite such powerful Conservative opposition, it was apparent by the close of the balloting in May, 1935, that the British people had spoken out in support of collective security. With an election in the offing, unless the government were to be at odds with the electorate, a change was obviously in order.[21]

Coinciding with the conclusion of the balloting, a dramatic cabinet shift took place. Increasingly frail both in physical health and political power, Ramsay MacDonald stepped down in favor of Stanley Baldwin. In his opening speech as Prime Minister, Baldwin announced major innovations clearly designed to win the support of those who had voted in the Peace Ballot. Sir John Simon, who had served as Foreign Secretary since the formation of the National government, was demoted to the Home Office. He had proved too outspoken against the referendum. His role in rearmament, the initiation of the Anglo-German Naval Agreement, the arms inquiry, and his attitude toward collective security were too well known. To ask the millions who had supported the Peace Ballot to accept a new statement of foreign policy from him was obviously impossible. Sir Samuel Hoare, fresh from triumphs at the India Office, became Foreign Secretary.[22]

To court Peace Ballot supporters, Baldwin created a new cabinet post. He named Anthony Eden Minister for League of Nations Affairs, thus establishing virtually a dual Secretariat. Although a few Liberals and Labourites might recall the new minister's hostility to the Peace Ballot, Eden had been unobtrusive in his attacks. Arguing that the League's moral authority must remain its strongest weapon, he had insisted that turning the world organization into a military machine would be a tragic mistake. He built a reputation as a young Conservative advocate of the League and collective security. His appointment therefore made the new government more palatable to ballot supporters.[23]

On June 27 Lord Cecil jubilantly announced the final referendum results. Originally hoping for at most five million votes, he was delighted that more than twice that number had participated. On question one: Should Great Britain remain a member of the League?, 96% of the voters replied emphatically in the affimative, and 91% favored an internationally negotiated armaments reduction. The poll showed that 82½% approved of the abolition of military aircraft and 90% favored the prohibition of armaments manufacture by private firms. The vote on the fifth question, however, appeared to prove Conservative contentions that the public did not understand the complexities involved. While 87% voted for economic or non-military sanctions, only 59% supported military sanctions.[24] The public did not yet understand what Baldwin had known in 1934: no sanctions would work unless backed by force. An interesting aspect of the vote was the sharp rise in the number of ballots cast in the spring of 1935. This undoubtedly reflected the tension created by the impending Italo-Ethiopian confrontation. Twelve million votes could not be ignored! The Conservatives quietly and quickly jettisoned their policy of pouring contumely on the Peace Ballot and its sponsors.[25] They turned their faces toward Geneva and bowed.

With a General Election approaching, Baldwin could not afford to disregard the significance of the vote. If the Peace Ballot shook his "boundless complacency," he concealed it when Lord Cecil presented him with the referendum figures. After listening to Cecil and others explain the origin, purpose, and results of the poll, Baldwin blandly reversed his previous stand, declaring that he welcomed so positive a reinforcement of the government's League policy. The world organization, he told his astonished audience, had always been the "sheet anchor" of British foreign policy and would continue to be so in the future.[26] Apparently his attitude toward collective security, so "perfectly impracticable" a few months earlier, had undergone a strange metamorphosis. Thus did this modern Moses lead the Conservatives out of the desert of political isolation into the promised land of twelve million votes. Apparently he and his government would henceforth follow what was in essence a new policy set by those who had voted on the Peace Ballot. If he failed to do so, electoral disaster lay ahead. A real change had taken place — or so it seemed.

On September 11 Sir Samuel Hoare dramatically stated the government's new policy at Geneva. His country accepted in full the obligations of League membership, he declared, for that membership formed the "oft proclaimed keynote" of British foreign policy. Referring to the Peace Ballot, he asserted that the "recent response" showed how completely public opinion supported the government's commitment to the League. No matter what the difficulties and pressures were in the Italo-Ethiopian dispute, he promised that the Conservative government would stand by the League.[27] Hoare's "magnificent" address was hailed as one of the finest in the history of the Assembly. His reference to the Peace Ballot impressed many who believed that the twelve million votes cast in the poll provided firm support for the government against Mussolini. Lord Cecil believed Sir Samuel had committed Baldwin's administration to "unequivocal" support of the Covenant and to action in the event of aggression in Ethiopia. Cecil discounted rumors from Geneva that the British government intended to "make a deal" with Italy as soon as a General Election was safely over.[28] But even as the audience applauded, the League was being betrayed—Hoare and Pierre Laval had met on the previous day and agreed that support for League principles must be held within narrow confines. This decision marked the beginning of what Hoare was pleased to call his "dual policy."

In effect, the dual policy was one of upholding the League, or appearing to uphold it sufficiently to impress the twelve million voters in Britain, while simultaneously dealing directly with Mussolini in an attempt to buy him off.[29] Until war actually broke out in Ethiopia, such a policy could be followed. After the invasion began, however, such a program became completely untenable. The dual policy had been adopted in response to the Peace Ballot, and Conservatives were caught in a dilemma from which no amount of words could extricate them.

In response to the Peace Ballot, the Conservatives found it expedient to pay lip service to the basic principles of the League. The declarations and actions of the Conservative government in the ensuing months, however, were at odds and created a dangerous dichotomy that undermined the effectiveness of the League of Nations.[30] Ultimately the Conservatives fatally vitiated the collective security system by publicly advocating a course which they could not, or would not, support privately. In their intense reaction to the Peace Ballot result, they set the stage in Geneva for the Italo-Ethiopian tragedy in which the British delegates acted out an unfamiliar role. Their performance won such warm applause that a General Election renewed the government's contract for five more years.[31]

Almost immediately, however, the warm glow of a resounding popular victory disappeared in the debacle of the Hoare-Laval Pact. The dual policy had resulted in "a disgraceful humiliation," which made the British Cabinet appear as dishonest "fools or knaves." The "weak and cowardly" handling of the Italo-Ethiopian affair seemed a treacherous desertion of both the League and the twelve million voters of the Peace Ballot.[32]

A timorous government, although recognizing the inconsistency of a vote that rejected rearmament while approving sanctions, nevertheless, failed to educate the British public to the realities of the international situation. Instead it stooped to duplicity and double-dealing, ultimately betraying not only the League but its own people. Born in idealism, the Peace Ballot had proved to be a unique but futile experiment in modern democracy and peace making. In tempting the Conservatives to say one thing and do another, those who conducted the referendum, including Robert Cecil, unwittingly contributed to the undermining of the institution they had so vainly sought to strengthen.

Notes

1. Great Britain, Public Record Office, Office of the Prime Minister, Premier 1/178, (Hereafter cited as P.R.O., Premier 1/178); *Parliamentary Debates, House of Lords*, 5th ser., XCV, 141-148; Edward Price Bell, "War Can Be Conquered, Cecil Believes," *Literary Digest* (January 26, 1935), 119:5, 33-34; Robert Cecil, *A Great Experiment* (New York: Oxford University Press, 1941), p. 259.
2. P.R.O., Premier 1/178; Cecil, *A Great Experiment*, pp. 257-258. A list of participating organizations may be found in the British Museum, Viscount Cecil of Chelwood Papers. For a history of the referendum's origins see Adelaide Livingston and Marjorie Scott Johnson, *The Peace Ballot: An Official History* (London: Victor Gollonces, Ltd., 1935).
3. University of Birmingham, Lady Katherine Dugdale to Sir Austen Chamberlain, November 9, 1934, Chamberlain Papers, AC 40/6/49; BM, Gilbert Murray to Cecil, November 16, 1934, Cecil Papers; *Parliamentary Debates, House of Commons*, 5th ser., CCLXXXXIII, 1315-1317; *Manchester Guardian*, July 25, and November 19, 1934; *Times* (London), November 23, 1934, and July 4, 1935; *The New York Times*, April 19, 1935.
4. *Times* (London), July 24 and 27, 1934.
5. University of Birmingham, Dugdale to Austen Chamberlain, November 9, 1934, Chamberlain Papers, AC 40/6/49; *Times* (London), November 13, 1934; *The New York Times*, December 16, 1934.
6. BM, Austen Chamberlain to Cecil, July 18, 1934, Cecil Papers; University of Birmingham, Austen Chamberlain to F. S. Oliver, August 3, 1933, Chamberlain Papers, AC 40/5/84; Dugdale to Austen Chamberlain, November 9, 1934, *ibid.*, AC 40/6/49; Robert, Viscount Cranborne to Austen Chamberlain, no date, *ibid.*, AC 40/6/50; a copy of a letter from Cranborne to Cecil, no date, *ibid*. See also *ibid.*, AC 40/6/7 a, b, c, d, e.
7. BM, Murray to Cecil, July 18, 1934, Cecil Papers.
8. *Parliamentary Debates, House of Commons*, 5th ser., CCLXXXXIII, 1345-1347; Bodleian Library, Oxford; Dorothea Layton to Murray, no date, Gilbert Murray Papers; Murray to Layton, November 14, 1931, *ibid.*
9. *Parlimentary Debates, House of Commons,* 5th ser., CCLXXXXIII,

1315-1317, 1345-1347; Bodleian Library, Layton to Murray, no date, Murray Papers; W. J. Pincombe to Sir John Simon, January 28,1941, Family Papers of John, Viscount Simon in the possession of the present Lord Simon. At the Foreign Office, Simon's view undoubtedly influenced the cold form letters sent out in reply to numerous requests for information on the government's attitude toward the Ballot. Lord Hutchinson of Montrose reportedly declared that his official opposition to the referendum had been "forced upon him by the Foreign Office," despite his sympathy with the poll. See BM, note of conversation with Sir John Simon and with Lord Hutchinson of Montrose, June 14, 1934, Cecil Papers; P.R.O., Foreign Office Minutes, 371 (1934) 71/14/98.

10. *Parliamentary Debates, House of Commons*, 5th ser., CCLXXXXIII, 888-889; *Times* (London), November 17 and 28, 1934.
11. *Manchester Guardian*, November 24, 1934; *Times* (London), November 24, 1931; University of Birmingham, Stanley Baldwin to Austen Chamberlain, February 17, 1933, Chamberlain Papers, AC 40/5/13.
12. *Times* (London), November 19, 1934 and July 8, 1935; P.R.O., Premier 1/178.
13. *Manchester Guardian*, November 14, 1934. See also Bodleian Library, correspondence of MacDonald and Murray, July, 1923, through June, 1924, Murray Papers.
14. *Times* (London), November 15, 1934. The *Times* poured scorn on the ballot almost continuously until June, 1935, as did numerous other journals. The *Daily Telegraph* (London), the *Daily Mail* (London), and the *Daily Express* (London), were particularly virulent.
15. BM, Maud, Countess of Selborne, to Cecil, July 2, 1934, Cecil Papers.
16. *Parliamentary Debates, House of Lords*, 5th ser., XCVI, 1036-1043; BM, Cecil to Countess of Selborne, July 3, 1934, Cecil Papers; Cecil to K. D. Courtney, June 2, 1934, *ibid.*; Cecil *A Great Experiment*, p. 257. Cecil was actually no longer active in party affairs and had sat on the cross benches of the House of Lords for some time. See BM, Cecil to Austen Chamberlain, December 19, 1935, Cecil Papers.
17. See the statement of Sir John Simon, *Parliamentary Debates, House of Commons*, 5th ser., CCLXXXXIII, 1315-1317; *Times* (London), November 23, 1934.
18. For a general background of the Crisis and its foreign policy repercussions see G. W. Baer, *The Coming of the Italian-Ethiopian War* (Cambridge, Massachusetts: Harvard University Press, 1967). Lord Harold Macmillan, *Winds of Change, 1914-1939* (New York and

Evanston: Harper & Row, Publishers, 1966), pp. 375-379; A. J. P. Taylor, *English History, 1914-1945* (New York and Oxford: Oxford University Press, 1965), pp. 379-381.

19. *Times* (London), November 24, 1934; *Manchester Guardian*, November 24, 1931.
20. *Parliamentary Debates, House of Commons*, 5th ser., CCLXXXXIII, 843.
21. *The New York Times*, April 19, 1935; *Times* (London), April 11, 1935.
22. Arnold Toynbee, (ed.), *Survey of International Affairs,* 1935, Vol. II, *Abyssinia and Italy* (London: Royal Institute of International Affairs, 1936), pp. 51-55. Cecil, *A Great Experiment*, pp. 259-261.
23. Cecil described Eden as "hostile" to the ballot. See BM, Cecil to Eden, December, 1934, Cecil Papers. See also *Times* (London), January 5, 1935; Stanley Baldwin, "England's Policy," *Vital Speeches* (July 15, 1935), 1: 667-668; Lewis Broad, *Sir Anthony Eden: The Chronicles of a Career* (London: Hutchinson, 1955), pp. 53-54. Alan Campbell-Johnson, *Eden: The Making of a Statesman* (New York: Ives Washburn, Inc., 1939, 1955), p. 112.
24. 357, 460 (3.1%) voted against remaining in the League and 867,227 (7.5%) were against a reduction of armaments, while 1,697,977 (14.6%) opposed a reduction of military aircraft. 779,513 (6.7%) voted against prohibition of armaments manufacture. On the last question, 638,211 (5.5%) opposed economic sanctions and 2,364,179 (20.3%) were against military sanctions. Abstentions and doubtfuls accounted for the remaining votes. See P.R.O. Premier 1/178 for a breakdown of votes.
25. Indications of a change can be seen throughout the spring in government attempts to conciliate the League of Nations Union which, according to Leslie Carruthers, was becoming "the diplomatic mouthpiece of the nation." See Bodleian Library, Leslie W. Carruthers to Murray, March 29, 1935, Murray Papers; R. Glynn to Murray, April 8, 9, 11, 1935, *ibid.* Murray believed that MacDonald's new "wish to be civil" to the Union was directly attributable to the ballot, Murray to Cecil, April 12, 1935, *ibid*. Toynbee, *Abyssinia and Italy*, p. 53, termed the government's shift "ludicrous."
26. P.R.O., Premier 1/178; *Times* (London), July 24, 1935; Campbell-Johnson, *Anthony Eden* (1939 ed.), p. 267.
27. Viscount Templewood (Sir Samuel Hoare), *Nine Troubled Years* (London: Hutchinson, 1954), p. 116. *Vital Speeches* (September 11, 1931), 1: 833-837.
28. Bodleian Library, Murray to Cecil, September 12, 1935, Murray Papers; BM, Courtney to Cecil, September 12, 1935, Cecil Papers;

Cecil to Courtney, September 16, 1935, *ibid.*; Mrs. T. W. Lamont to Cecil, no date, *ibid.*; Cecil to Lamont, December 6, 1935, *ibid.*; Cecil to Murray, November 6, 1935, *ibid.*; *The New York Times*, July 14, 1935; *Times* (London), September 16, October 11, 1935.

29 Templewood, *Nine Troubled Years*, p. 116.

30. Toynbee, *Abyssinia and Italy*, pp. 53-55; Cecil, *A Great Experiment*, p. 260.

31. Macmillan, *Winds of Change*, pp. 375-379.

32. Beaverbrook Library, Philip Snowden to Lloyd George, January 3, 1936, Papers of David Lloyd George, G 18/7/14; BM, Margot Asquith (Lady Oxford) to Cecil, December 11, 1935, Cecil Papers.